T H E
GODS
were
ASTRONAUTS

THE
GODS
were
ASTRONAUTS

The Extraterrestrial Identity of the Old Gods Revealed

Erich von Däniken

This edition first published in 2023 by New Page Books, an imprint of

Red Wheel/Weiser, LLC
With offices at:
65 Parker Street, Suite 7
Newburyport, MA 01950
www.redwheelweiser.com

All the Bible quotes are from the standard King James Bible, the Old and New Testaments.

ISBN: 978-1-63748-000-7

Library of Congress Cataloging-in-Publication Data

Names: Däniken, Erich von, 1935- author. | Däniken, Erich von, 1935- Götter waren Astronauten!
Title: The gods were astronauts : the extraterrestrial identity of the old gods revealed / Erich von Däniken.
Other titles: Götter waren Astronauten! English
Description: Newburyport, MA : New Page Books, [2023] | "Previously published in English 2002 by Vega, ISBN: 9781843336259"–Colophon. | Includes bibliographical references and index. | Summary: This book propounds-and offers persuasive evidence-that the winged angels populating the Bible, Koran, and other religious texts from cultures the world over were in reality extraterrestrials who visited the Earth in ages long past. Intellectually challenging and provocative, these findings may shake the foundations of both science and faith"– Provided by publisher.
Identifiers: LCCN 2023001360 | ISBN 9781637480007 (trade paperback) | ISBN 9781633412422 (ebook)
Subjects: LCSH: Civilization, Ancient–Extraterrestrial influences. | Space theology. | BISAC: BODY, MIND & SPIRIT / Ancient Mysteries & Controversial Knowledge | BODY, MIND & SPIRIT / Supernatural (incl. Ghosts)
Classification: LCC CB156 .D33413 2023 | DDC 001.942–dc23/eng/20230113
LC record available at https://lccn.loc.gov/2023001360

Cover design by Sky Peck Design
Cover art adapted from Dante's *Paradiso*, Gustave Dore, 1870
Interior by Happenstance Type-O-Rama
Typeset in Franklin Gothic Std, ITC New Baskerville Std, Orpheus Pro, and Warnock Pro

Printed in the United States of America
IBI
10 9 8 7 6 5 4 3 2 1

TABLE OF CONTENTS

INTRODUCTION
TO THE NEW EDITION

IT ALL STARTED IN 1966 with *Chariots of the Gods?* At the time I claimed that the gods of mythology and ancient religions were actually astronauts from distant solar systems. Critics raised legitimate questions: Are there any extraterrestrials at all? What could they look like? How did they bridge the light years from star to star and in general: Why should they have visited Earth?

More than fifty years have passed since then. There are now logical and convincing answers to most questions. Countless ancient texts have been newly translated and interpreted in a modern way. Former "angels" became extraterrestrials, "heaven" became the universe, and battles in the firmament became battles in space. Fifty years ago, the "gods" were considered to be fantasy figures. It was thought that our Stone Age ancestors had deified the forces of nature—the thunder, the lightning, the earthquake—and so natural religions came into being. That is certainly correct, and yet it is not enough to explain the experiences described in old, holy books. For example, a person named Enoch is taken into space before the flood. He learns the language of foreigners, is instructed in the art of writing, and then several professionals teach him geology, engineering, and astronomy. One of the teachers asks Enoch: "Son of man, look out. Do you see that little light out there? You humans say 'Moon' to it, but the moon has no light of its own, it draws its light from the sun. . . ." Then the phases of the moon and the earthly calendar are explained to Enoch. He is taught that the Earth revolves around the Sun in 365 days.

The previous explanations are no longer sufficient for such information. After all, Enoch lived before the flood; he was a man of the Stone Age. He could not know anything about the phases of the Moon, much less about the planetary orbit of the Earth around the Sun. Information flowed. Scientific information. And it cannot come from a force of nature such as an earthquake, a volcanic eruption, or a thunderstorm. The ancient gods were real.

That's what this book is all about. I analyze the old, holy, and also less holy scriptures—examine them for contradictions and experiences that clearly indicate a visit by strange astronauts. So also the belief in the return of some savior across cultures and religions to this day. Those gods had promised thousands of years ago that they would one day return to our Earth. This expectation of a return haunts all religions to this day. And meanwhile the gods have come again.

In this book I use the example of the so-called appearances of Fátima in Portugal. At that time, in 1917, three shepherd children experienced an alleged apparition of the Mother of God, and 80,000 people witnessed a so-called solar miracle. They saw a glowing disk in the firmament, which changed color and showed itself for a total of a full eight minutes. The

Catholic Church conjured up an apparition of the Mother of God from it. I can prove that none of this is true and that all popes have known about extraterrestrials since 1917 and that their believers are not telling the truth about Fátima.

The aim of this book is to fascinate the reader and to give them thoughts that they can control themselves. Most of the time, a copy of the Bible is enough.

Erich von Däniken
April 15, 2022

INTRODUCTION

IT WAS SOME SEVENTY-FIVE years ago, and it happened in the primary school of the town of Schaffhausen in Switzerland. I was about ten years old and listened to our religious instructor telling us that once a battle had taken place in Heaven. One day the archangel Lucifer had appeared before the throne of God with his legion of angels and had declared, "We are not going to serve you any more!" At which point the Almighty God had ordered the archangel Michael to chuck Lucifer out of Heaven, along with all his rebellious followers. Michael duly carried out this command with his flaming sword. From that day—according to our religious education (R.E.) teacher—Lucifer had become the Devil and all his followers were burning in Hell.

That evening, for the first time in my young life, I was really pensive. We children had been told that Heaven was a place of absolute bliss, a place where all the good people went after they died. A place too where all souls became intimately one with God. How could conflict occur in such paradisiacal realms? Where absolute joy ruled, where oneness with God was perfect, there could be no opposition, no quarrel. Why, oh why, should Lucifer and all his angels suddenly rebel against an almighty, all-loving God?

My mother, whom I asked for an explanation, was unable to help. With God, she said, wearing a troubled expression, everything was possible. That's how it had to be. Even the impossible.

Later, at high school, where we were taught Latin, I understood that the name *Lucifer* was formed out of the two words *lux* (light) and *ferre* (to do, to carry). Lucifer really means Lightmaker or Bringer of Light. Of all creatures, was the Devil supposed to be the Bringer of Light? My realization, based on the Latin, made the whole business even more bewildering.

Twenty years later, I had thoroughly studied the Old Testament, as Christians call the ancient traditions. There I read passages from the Jewish prophet Isaiah (c. 740 BC):

> *How art thou fallen from heaven, O Lucifer, son of the morning! How art thou cut down to the ground, which didst weaken the nations! For thou hast said in thine heart, I will ascend into heaven, I will exalt my throne above the stars of God: I will sit also upon the mount of the congregation . . . (Isaiah 14:12–13)*

These verses from Isaiah may have been altered during the course of the millennia. But what might he have been thinking about originally? In the so-called "Revelation" of John (author of the prophecy of the apocalypse), one can read another clear and definite allusion to battles in Heaven in chapter 12, verse 7:

> *And there was war in heaven: Michael and his angels fought against the dragon; and the dragon fought and his angels, and prevailed not; neither was their place found any more in heaven.*

Curious. The great traditions of other peoples, too, support the idea that these battles in heaven were not entirely made up. In the Egyptian Book of the Dead, a collection of texts that were placed in a grave with a mummified body so the deceased would know how to behave in the Beyond, we read how Ra, the mighty Sun god, fought against the rebellious children of heaven. The god Ra, we read, never left his "egg" during the entire battle.[1]

Battles in Heaven? In outer space? Or did our ignorant forefathers merely mean the battles between good and evil that are fought within humans? Did they perhaps imagine the atmospheric battle during a thunderstorm and project it on to a battle in outer space? A battle of dark clouds against the Sun? Or did the origin of this bewildering thinking lie in a solar eclipse, where something terrible was trying to eat up the Sun? All these natural explanations do not really take us any further, as I will demonstrate. If the battle between Lucifer and Michael were only to be found in the ancient Jewish sphere, one could easily gloss over it. But it is not the only example, and very old stories only too often show up astonishing similarities.

For thousands of years, Tibetan monasteries preserved texts called *dzyan*. Some original text, which may or may not still exist, must have been the source of the many *dzyan* fragments that have turned up in Indian temple libraries. We are talking of hundreds of sheets written in Sanskrit, sandwiched between two pieces of wood. There, one can read that in the "fourth world age," the sons were ordered to create likenesses of themselves. A third of the sons refused to carry out the command:

> *The older wheels turned down and up. The spawn of the Mother filled the All. Battles were fought between the creators and the destroyers, and battles about Space . . . Do your calculations, Lanoo, if you wish to obtain the true age of your wheel.* (author's emphasis)[2]

I discussed parts of Greek mythology in my last book.[3] Greek mythology also begins with a battle in heaven. The children of Ouranos rebelled against the heavenly order and the creator. Terrible battles ensued, and Zeus, the Father of the gods, is only *one* of the victors. Prometheus was one of those who fought against Zeus, and this took place in "Heaven," as Prometheus was the one who stole the fire from Heaven and brought it down to Earth. Prometheus— Lucifer. The Bringer of Light?

On the other side of the world, far from Greece, lies New Zealand. Even 135 years ago, ethnologist John White was asking the old priests of the Maori about their legends. Their legends too begin with a battle in Heaven.[4] Some of the sons of God rebelled against their father. The leader of these space warriors was called Ronga-mai, and after a victorious battle, he allowed himself to be feted on Earth.

His appearance was like a brilliant star, like a flame, like a sun. Wherever he landed, the Earth was churned up, dust clouds obscured one's view, the noise sounded like thunder and, from a distance, like the rushing sound inside a sea shell.

These accounts cannot just be disposed of by shoving them into the psychologist's bag. A very ancient memory has been preserved here. In the Drona Parva,[5] the oldest Indian tradition, the battles in space are described in the same manner as in old Jewish legends that are not part of the Old Testament.[6] There too there is mention of "holy wheels," "in which the cherubim reside." This is, of course, not just anywhere, but "in Heaven" and "among the stars."

Etymologists assure us that one should see all this symbolically.[7] These strange stories are only myths.[8] Only? Which family tree should we climb up, then, if all that is to be found in mythology are symbols? And if they are symbols, what do the symbols stand for? The term *symbol* comes from the Greek *symballein* and means "to throw together." If myths are only to be perceived symbolically, I would really like to know what exactly has been "thrown together." An attempt to side with the vagueness of myths will not take us one step further. We have become a society that simply accepts and believes the most contradictory traditions, believing in the way religions would have us believe. But evidently we are not prepared to accept a few facts. When I maintain that the Holy Book, and the first books of the Old Testament in particular, bristle with contradictions and horror stories, and that the God who spoke to Moses could never be looked upon as the true God of Creation, people become offended and indignantly demand proof. When I present the evidence, I get publicly clobbered for my pains. Why? Because we are not supposed to question beliefs and faith. Of course, that only applies to the beliefs of the larger religious groups. If I attack the beliefs of a smaller group, the rule no longer applies.

Mankind has arrived in a new millennium. For myself, I think it is more responsible to analyze the old stories and target new goals.

CHAPTER 1

A Different Kind of R.E. Lesson

Science is the only remedy against superstition.
—HENRY T. BUCKLE

THERE IS NO ARGUING about the fact that human beings doubt and even despair of God. Everyone is familiar with the question: How could God let it happen? It might refer to the millions of maltreated and murdered Jews in the Second World War or to the torture victims of all dictatorships. How could God allow innocent children to be tortured and killed? How can he permit natural catastrophes that bring starvation and suffering to so many peoples? How could he allow Christians to be persecuted in his name; allow humans to be slaughtered in dreadful ways; allow Christian zealots to put other Christians, witches, or those allegedly possessed by the Devil to death by unimaginable, atrocious methods of torture? The list of questions, about how God could have allowed all these things, is endless—and the answers, which we swallow along with the incomprehensible, are always the same. God has, so we are talked into believing, reserved a special place in Heaven for those maltreated victims. There, in that kingdom beyond, they will be well rewarded. God's counsel is incomprehensible but wise. Man thinks but God guides. We should not pose questions about the "why," credulous theologians assure us. God alone knows "why."

Maybe. But this same God—so the Christian, Jewish, and Muslim tradition goes—is supposed to have created us "in his own image." We read this in Genesis, and it is valid for the three great world religions:

> *And God said, Let us make man in our image, after our likeness; and let them have dominion over the fish of the sea, and over the fowl of the air, and over the cattle, and over all the earth, and over every creeping thing that creepeth upon the earth. So God created man in his own image, in the image of God he created him; male and female created he them. (Genesis 1:26–27; author's emphasis)*

If man is the image or likeness of God, he should also be intelligent. And no one could dispute that what we understand as God must be the highest of all imaginable intelligences. Intelligent life forms just happen to have the habit of asking questions and searching for answers. Intelligent beings do not believe in any old nonsense. And if we are *not* in God's image, we are still left with the fact that we are intelligent beings, either with or without "God's image." Here, by "intelligence," I mean culture in the widest possible sense, something that separates us from animals. And there is another thing: God should be not only the power of intelligence to the highest degree but naturally infallible as well. But the God we meet in the Old Testament is not infallible. After God created man and woman, he saw: "it was very good" (Genesis 1:31). That is what one would expect from divine work. But this same Lord, who created man, shortly afterward regretted what he had done:

> And it repented the Lord that he had made man on the earth, and it grieved him at his heart. And the Lord said, I will destroy man whom I have created from the face of the earth; both man, and beast, and the creeping thing, and the fowls of the air; for it repenteth me that I have made them. (Genesis 6:6)

Incomprehensible! First, this infallible God creates animals and man, discovers that it is good, and then he repents of his deed. This is divine?

A further characteristic that has to be attributed to God is timelessness. A true God must stand outside time. He would never have to try out experiments and then wait to see how they turn out. But this is exactly what happens in the Old Testament, several times. After God created man, he set them down in the Garden of Eden. There, Adam and Eve were allowed to do anything they liked except for one thing: they were not allowed to eat the apple. It is beside the point whether the apple stands as a symbol for something else: whether for sin or the first sexual act. A prohibition exists. This timeless God should have known from the start that his creations would circumvent this prohibition—which is exactly what happens, whereupon the deeply offended God chases our first ancestors out of Paradise. The Christian Church has even managed to top this with further illogical concepts: all the descendants of Adam and Eve are saddled with an ominous "original sin" that can be paid off only by the blood sacrifice of God's only son. A truly dreadful thought.

I am—and I repeat this in each of my books—a believer in God and a God-fearing person. I pray too, every day. My poor brain is not capable of defining God. Many cleverer people than I have tried to—and still, for me, God is something quite extraordinary and certainly unique. I am in agreement with the great world religions: there can be only one God. And that which we call God must be infallible, timeless, omnipresent, and omnipotent. Those are the very least characteristics we have to concede to God with deep respect. It will never be possible to describe God or to nail down the Holy Spirit anywhere on a timeline.

Science tells us, at the beginning, hydrogen was all there was, or the Big Bang. And what caused the Big Bang? What was before the Big Bang? This Big Bang, the super-clever astrophysicists tell us, happened about 15,000 million years ago and lasted a fraction of a second. But we are unable to explain that fraction of a second. Nothing arises from nothing—even the most intricate mathematical formulas will not overcome that obstacle.

Albert Einstein (1879–1955), in addition to the theory of relativity, also formulated the lesser-known theory of gravitation. Both explain the macrocosm, our "greater universe," so to speak. Then along came another genius from the field of physics, Werner Heisenberg (1901–1976), who developed formulas of quantum physics, which to this day can only be understood by specialists. The behavior of the microcosm can be explained with the help of quantum physics. What is going on behind those subatomic particles? To be exact, both concepts—the gravitation theory and quantum physics—should meet in the Big Bang theory. But the mathematical theories that attempt to connect the two concepts turn out to be just absurd numbers and formulas that do not make sense. Nothing seems to fit together. A plausible theory that would presumably be called "quantum gravitation" does not exist. The breeding chamber of the universe has remained locked. Space and time, which supposedly did not exist before the Big Bang, came into being at the same time as the Big Bang. But what did exist *before* space and time began to be?

Space and time came into being simultaneously, as our needle-sharp, analytical astrophysicists' minds have discovered. Innumerable calculations were carried out and computers fed with data to arrive at this epoch-making realization. International conferences were organized and deeply meaningful papers were read. Scientists could have arrived at the answer much more easily. Plato's *Timaeus* dialogue, written about 2,500 years ago, tells us:

> *So time then came into being with the heavens in order that, having come into being together, they should also be dissolved together if ever they are dissolved . . .*[1]

If we start with the question "What is God?" we could equally well ask, "Who (or what) created God?" There is no end—or better, no beginning. Human beings made a father figure out of God, a person who commands and punishes, praises and criticizes. This is certainly not what Creation is about. Theologians argue that we should grant this creator being the ability to be able to transform into a person at any moment and to take on human form. That may well be. But even then, this God-Person should retain its divine attributes. Naturally, I am familiar with concepts of God from different religions and philosophical schools, and in the end, they all boil down to the same thing: whatever God is, "it" should be eternal, timeless, perfect, and omnipresent. It was Albert Einstein who coined the phrase "God does not play dice with the universe."

The one in the Old Testament did. And in several demonstrable cases he did not foresee the future, as can be seen, for example, with regard to the prophet Ezra (Hebrew: succor). Ezra was one of the few prophets who returned to Jerusalem around 458 BC, after the Babylonian captivity.

In the Old Testament, there is just one chapter about Ezra, but the apocryphal texts contain much more about him. There we find Ezra asking God—or his emissaries—about the signs that would come and about his own life. The answer was as follows:

I can only tell you about some of the signs you ask about. I am not able to tell you anything about your future life, as I do not know myself.[2] *(author's emphasis)*

Now, Ezra did not belong in the same period as Moses, and it may be that he was having his conversations with somebody else, only not with God. But the God of Adam and Eve's times did not seem to know what was going on either. After Eve had served up the apple to her husband, he hid himself in the bushes "out of fear." But God did not seem to know where Adam was:

> And the Lord God called unto Adam, and said unto him, Where art thou? (Genesis 3:9)

Adam assured the Lord that he had heard him but had hidden himself because he was "ashamed." Then, the Lord wanted to know who had told Adam he was naked and asked whether he had eaten of the tree that was forbidden. Adam replied:

> The woman who thou gavest to be with me, she gave me of the tree, and I did eat. (Genesis 3:12)

According to this version, God was definitely not in the picture. He did not know where Adam was and had no idea that Eve had tempted him to eat the apple. People who believe the Bible say that such passages should not be taken literally; everything should be seen symbolically. Well, all right then, but even the "symbolic illogic" does not make sense, as we shall see.

After Adam worked out how to have sex, Eve bore her sons Cain and Abel. Abel became a shepherd, and Cain became an arable farmer—two crisis-proof, subsidized professions. The two boys brought sacrifices before the Lord. And what did this infallible God do? He acknowledged Abel and his sacrifice with a well-pleased eye but did not acknowledge Cain and his sacrifice (Genesis 4:4–5).

Up to this point neither Cain nor Abel had any experience of double standards. No wonder Cain reacted in a disgruntled way to this partisan God:

And the Lord said unto Cain, Why art thou wroth, and why is thy countenance fallen? (Genesis 4:6)

An all-knowing God should have known. But this one did not even prevent Cain from killing his innocent brother, Abel. He even had to ask:

And the Lord said unto Cain, Where is Abel thy brother? And he says: I know not: am I my brother's keeper? (Genesis 4:9)

Although "God" ended up punishing Cain, the latter was still destined to become the progenitor of a phenomenally large lineage that was to make biblical history. But Cain was not the only murderer in God's eyes, as the much later Moses carried the same stigma. I will come back to Moses later.

The biblical narrative begins to turn decidedly dramatic in chapter 6:

And it came to pass, when men began to multiply on the face of the earth, and daughters were born unto them, that the sons of God saw the daughters of men that they were fair; and they took wives of all which they chose . . .

There were giants in the earth in those days; and also after that, when the sons of God came in unto the daughters of men, and they bare children to them, the same became mighty men which were of old, men of renown. (Genesis 6:4)

I shall not discuss those giants any more, as I have already done so in a previous book.[3] The question of those "sons of

God" has also come up before.[4] I just do not comprehend how those who believe in the Bible, and who usually quote all manner of passages from the Holy Book, always seem to ignore these crucial passages. Yet, it is quite clear that what is spoken of is "the sons of God." I can nowadays only manage a weary smile in the face of the scholarly battles that have raged for centuries around these words and resulted in thousands of contradictory comments. Here, the term *sons of God* has been translated as "fallen angels"; there, they have been interpreted as "renegade spirit beings" or as "Guardians of the Heavens." It's enough to make one tear out one's hair! Three little words have twisted Faith into its opposite. The experts who are able to read Hebrew, however, know exactly what these three words are referring to—"those who descended from above."

In the end, this conflict among theologians about the meaning of the term *sons of God* is irrelevant. Whether they are interpreted as "rebel angels" or "Guardians of Heaven," God should have known beforehand what they were up to. Evidently, he had no idea. And those who would like to make "spirit beings" out of these "sons of God" should read on in the Holy Book. These spirit beings have sex with humans. Spirits do not do this.

Confusion reigns supreme in the Book of Genesis. The thing that saddens me is that millions of people believe that this contradictory God spoken of in Genesis is identical with the grandiose Spirit who created the universe. And this is not just in popular belief—no, even in theological specialist literature, which twists and justifies every contradiction with unbelievable sophistry, the God of the Old Testament is seen as the universal, only God with all the divine attributes.

Famous Jesuit and professor of theology Karl Rahner, who teaches whole hosts of young priests, assures us that the story of the Old Testament "originates from *the* God who, in the end, revealed himself in Jesus Christ."[5] The text of the Old and New Testaments, according to Rahner, all have the same source. God "has made a special covenant" with the people of Israel, which from "time immemorial" has, however, been planned as a mere prologue to the coming of Christ. Oh, and the Old Testament was planned right from the beginning as an "open movement, steered by God, towards final salvation."

The very inventive and wordy theology professors do concede that the Old Testament has been cobbled together out of diverse texts that originate from different times and are by various authors. Patriarchal reports originating from the dim and distant past had been collected together. They even admit to "artistic license" from various theological schools, all according to the needs of their time. For example, there is the insinuation that the histories of Israel, such as those of the Yahvists or those of the descendants of King David, were only aimed at legitimizing Solomon's throne or the takeover of Palestine by Israel. In the face of such claims, there is no need to be surprised that Jews and Christians find it so hard to get on. In spite of all these concessions and twists of interpretation, a kind of abstruse know-all attitude prevails in theological circles, which maintains that the historical narratives in the Bible are "without exception reports of the consummation of the Word of God. This formula is universally applicable." The latter statement is according to theology professor Jacques Guillet.[6]

So, how is this supposed to look? The Old Testament is supposed to be "a movement, directed by God, towards ultimate salvation" (Rahner). This plan is "universally applicable" (Guillet). And so that there may be no doubts at all, the story of the Old Testament and the New Testament originates from a single God, who revealed himself in Christ, "so that the text of the Old and New Testaments should have the same source" (Rahner). At the same time, many of the patriarchal reports are supposed to have originated "in the dim and distant past" and still be "without exception, reports of the consummation of God's Word."

The only remedy for this highbrow theological nonsense is probably education. One should not presume to tell me what I should be seeing. I *am* able to read.

The story of the Deluge and Noah's Ark is generally well known, and I have dealt with it in previous books. For those of you who are new to my books, I will merely repeat; what you read about the Deluge in Genesis chapter 6, verse 9, originates from much older Babylonian and even Sumerian texts.[7,8] Somebody in the distant past has, therefore, inserted a story into the Book of Books, the Holy Writ, and also invented the name Noah; and all of this originates from completely different sources. And still—according to theology—the Old Testament deals "without exception with reports of the consummation of the Word of God" (Jacques Guillet).

After the Great Flood, and when the Ark landed on top of a mountain, Noah made a sacrifice to the Lord, and according to Genesis chapter 8, verse 21: "And the Lord smelled a sweet savor." This is not very different from what happens in the Epic of Gilgamesh. Utnapishtim, who survived the Flood, sacrificed a lamb, grain, cedar wood, and myrtle on the mountain: "The gods smelled the odor, and the odor rose pleasantly to the nostrils of the gods. And the gods assembled like flies around the sacrifice."[9]

Strange gods, who are able to smell frying meat!

After this pleasant odor of cooked meat, the God of the Old Testament decided that he would "not again curse the ground any more for man's sake" (Genesis 8:21). And also "neither will I again smite any more every living thing, as I have done." He invited Noah and his sons to be fruitful and to multiply and replenish the Earth. God also stated clearly that all animals should be subject to man:

> And the fear of you and the dread of you shall be upon every beast of the earth, and upon every fowl of the air, and all that moveth upon the earth, and upon all the fishes of the sea; into your hands are they delivered. (Genesis 9:2)

Animal lovers will probably never be able to follow comfortably this divine command. In the older parallel story from the Epic of Gilgamesh, several gods smelled the frying meat and gathered above the Ark. The gods began to squabble with each other and harangue the god Enlil, who caused the Flood. "O wisest of gods, O great warrior hero, how could you, taking no counsel, bring on the Deluge?"[10]

In the end, "the God of the earth and all lands" climbed "into the ship," led Utnapishtim together with his wife out of the Ark, laid his hands on them, and blessed them. (An additional Flood story with a similar content is described in the *Enuma elish*, from the Babylonian "tutelary poem of the Creation."[11])

Whoever it was who was identified as God in these sources, he was definitely not the Creator of the Universe. The Old Testament and the Epic of Gilgamesh describe the same events, however, with the decided difference that, in the Epic of Gilgamesh an eyewitness is featured who writes the report in the first person. Utnapishtim is the survivor of the Flood, just like Noah in the Bible, but in the latter, the story is told in the third person.

The God of the Old Testament too blessed his protégés and sealed an "eternal covenant" with them and for all their descendants:

And the waters shall no more become a flood to destroy all flesh.
(Genesis 9:15)

Really, that is rather a reassuring statement, if it actually came from the mouth of God. Earth-dwellers of all times should never have to fear the effects of a meteorite strike in the sea. As astronomers today are aware, such strikes are quite possible, with terrifyingly destructive consequences for all humankind. But this promise does not actually originate from the Creator of the Universe, from that incomprehensible intelligence of the first source. The ancient texts in the Gilgamesh epic and in the Old Testament speak of other gods. Gods? Surely, the Old Testament speaks only of *one* God? I have already had to destroy this illusion in my previous books. The Hebrew word that stands for "God" in Genesis is *elohim*. This is a plural word. There is no singular *elohim*. What is meant is "the gods." This though may be sobering, but it remains the truth.

The Jewish, Islamic, and Christian world religions are based on the books of Genesis. Islam treats the old stories of Moses and Solomon (Suleiman) as respectful traditions. The Torah scholars of the Jewish world religion not only have always been believers but have also seen their traditions as subjects of interpretation and research, and their work can be read, for example, in the many *midrash* volumes. These literary works known as *midrashim* contain the research of many centuries of outstanding Jewish scholars. A *midrash* is a work of interpretation, a search for meaning.[12, 13] It is only the Christian religion that constructs the "Word of God" out of the Old Testament texts, "generally applicable and without exception reports of the consummation of a Word of God" (Rahner).

Now, no religion just "appears." Every religion has a history, a kind of *Ur-Religion,* as humans were supposed to be able to keep to and live according to the pronouncements of their forefathers. There is no written evidence of this earliest religion. It probably took centuries for the various stories to be compressed into a Story. Each of these stories will presumably contain a kernel of truth, but to designate all these stories together as the "Word of God" comes close to an insult to the Infinite Power of Creation (provided, of course, that the intelligence behind Creation can be insulted by such microscopic creations as humans). The traditions collected together in the Old Testament do talk of gods who were active some time and somewhere, but they do not fit under the umbrella of an intelligent original spirit.

The God of the Old Testament, in fact, created several "eternal covenants" with Abraham (Genesis 13:15; Genesis 15:5; Genesis 15:18). *One* really divine covenant would have been sufficient. Again and again, burnt offerings and tribute were demanded. I find it quite inexplicable that a metaphysical God should have required them. Then there is the rather unsavory story of Sodom and Gomorrah. It appears like blasphemy to attribute that event to the intelligent creative power of God.

First of all, the biblical God heard that people were committing horrible sins in Sodom and Gomorrah. But he did not seem to be certain: "I will go down now, and see whether they have done altogether according to the cry of it, which is come unto me" (Genesis 18:21). God hadn't a clue. Very sad. Then God informed Abraham of what he intended to do, and Abraham began to plead with him. This is divine? Finally, God sent two angels to Sodom to save Lot and his family from the destruction of the two cities (Genesis 19:1 ff). To begin with, these angels intended to spend the night in a public place (why do angels need to sleep?), but Lot implored them not to do this and to come and rest in his house. This evidently did not suit the lustful mob of Sodom, and immediately they surrounded Lot's house and demanded the two angels be handed over to them, "that we may know them." The pressure must have been great, as Lot offered the lecherous people his two virgin daughters: "Do ye to them as is good in your eyes." The sodomites were not interested. They began to charge Lot's house and break down the door. Now, at last, the angels intervened. With some kind of secret weapon, they "smote the men that were at the door of the house with blindness, both small and great, so that they wearied themselves to find the door" (Genesis 19:11 ff). The situation came dramatically to a head. The two angels pressured Lot and his family to leave the city immediately. Lot was still hesitating. The angels became forceful. They dragged Lot, his wife, and two daughters out of the house:

Escape for thy life; look not behind thee, neither stay thou in all the plain; escape to the mountain, lest thou be consumed. (Genesis 19:17)

Lot's family forced to leave Sodom.

In spite of this urgent appeal, Lot was still complaining. Instead of fleeing to the hills, he insisted on staying in the little town of Zoar because he would feel safer there. Resigned to his stubbornness, the angels declared:

Haste thee, escape thither; for I cannot do any thing till thou be come thither. (Genesis 19:22)

But the Lord—the good Lord?—caused fire and brimstone to rain on Sodom and Gomorrah, "from the Lord out of heaven: and he overthrew those cities, and all the plain, and all the inhabitants of the cities, and that which grew upon the ground."

Evidently, a rather wayward brood was flourishing in the cities of Sodom and Gomorrah. But should the all-knowing God not have known beforehand what was going on? And why the sudden haste, the extreme pressure? Was there a countdown running, which neither the angels nor God could stop? What kind of a God was this?

My little Bible lesson is not intended to do anything more or less than make a certain observation: a god figure is described here who makes mistakes, errs, feels regret, is capable of bloody acts of destruction, and is not timeless. All of these are non-divine attributes that do not go with the perception of a being that stands above all things. It is also no use demanding a definition of God here because the Old Testament tells the story this way and in no other. Humans are encouraged to believe that these narratives are God's word.

Just in passing: the destruction of Sodom and Gomorrah was not the only destruction of sinful cities. The Indian epic Mahabharata tells the same story with a few special ingredients:[14] with chagrin one reads about a weapon that caused the city and its entire surroundings to be burned out completely. A horrific sight presented itself: the corpses no longer looked like those of human beings; the burnt bodies were unrecognizable. All food had become toxic, and never before had human beings seen such a terrible weapon, let alone heard of it.

While the destruction of Sodom and Gomorrah is described in two sentences, the account in the eighth book of the Mahabharata is more detailed. In both cases, a god was responsible for the dreadful destruction. The God of all religions? I am not so concerned with understanding the old accounts, sentence by sentence, word for word. These are concepts from a very distant past. Some god or the other, or gods, got nasty, broke off a failed experiment, or supported a preferred group of humans with their superior weapons.

These gods always came from heaven or the sky. The standard assumption—that our ancestors must have placed their perceived gods in the heavens because the heavens with the stars stood for the eternal or the unattainable—does not stand up to any kind of critical analysis, as there were plenty of figures that came from the darkness of the underworld. The descriptions of these battles of the gods in the heavens and the behavior of those heavenly beings on Earth are not explainable either poetically or psychologically. In addition to that, the descriptions are much too precise. Also, these heavenly beings spoke. They gave advice, commands, and often instructions of a technical nature.

The God of the Old Testament provides excellent examples of this. He demanded the sacrifice of Abraham's only son "whom thou lovest" (Genesis 22). Shortly before the terrible deed can be carried out, God sent an angel from Heaven to prevent this incomprehensible act. Theologians explain this contradiction as a test. God wanted to see whether Abraham would be prepared to slaughter his only son for God. He should have known this before. As a reward for this non-deed, which was only prevented by the intervention of an angel, God blessed Abraham and promised to make his descendants as numerous as "the stars of the heaven, and as the sand which is upon the sea shore" (Genesis 22:17). This is a promise that, in its first phase, could only be realized by polygamy. There is plenty of polygamy in the Book of Genesis (examples: Genesis, chapters 25, 29, and 34).

In the second Book, called Exodus, the main part is played by Moses. A man from the house of Levi had married a Levite woman, who gave birth to a pretty boy child. Three months after his birth, the mother could no longer hide the child from the Egyptians and wove a basket out of reeds, into which she laid the child. Naturally, the basket was made watertight with pitch and bitumen. One of Pharaoh's daughters pulled the basket out of the Nile and adopted the child.

This touching story originally, however, could have taken place in India. We find the same story in the Book called Adi Parva of the Mahabharata. The unmarried young woman Kunti had been waylaid by the Sun god, and the result of this unusual union was a son who was unusually beautiful because his face shone like the Sun. The former virgin Kunti feared the scandal, so she made a watertight casket and secretly abandoned the small child to the river. A courageous woman called Adhirata fished the casket out of the water, brought up the child as her own, and called him Karna.

A third story with the very same content was literally dug up in the nineteenth century from the hill of Kuyunyik, the former Nineveh, by Professor George Smith. British archaeologists uncovered an entire library of clay tablets that belonged to the Assyrian king Assurbanipal, and that included, among other things, the life story of King Sargon I (c. 2400 BC). He too, so the story goes, was laid in a reed basket secured with pitch and floated down the Euphrates. This strange little boat was found by a water carrier called Akki, and the little boy was finally brought up by a princess. About 1,000 years lie between the story of Sargon and the one about Moses. But just how many years lie between the story of the Indian virgin Kunti and the story of Moses, we cannot now determine.

God's word? Who copied it from whom?

After Moses grew up, he watched his Hebrew brothers performing the work of slaves. He was witness to a killing of a Hebrew by an Egyptian foreman:

> And he looked this way and that way, and when he saw that there was no man, he slew the Egyptian, and hid him in the sand. (Exodus 2:12)

The following day Moses watched two Hebrews quarreling. Moses tried to mediate, but one Hebrew answered:

> "Who made thee a prince and a judge over us? Intendest thou to kill me, as thou killedst the Egyptian?"

Moses was afraid, as his murder of the day before appeared to be public knowledge. He fled to the land of Midian, took as his wife the young daughter of (allegedly) a priest, and begat his first son, Gershon, with her. No special role appears to have been intended for the latter in the Bible, as with one exception (Exodus 18:2 ff), he disappears again without a trace.

While Moses was tending his father-in-law's sheep, he came to the sacred mountain called Horeb and watched the strange spectacle of flames burning in a thornbush without the bush being consumed. Curious, Moses moved closer, and to his astonishment heard a voice coming from the thornbush. The voice commanded him to take off his shoes and step closer, as he was on holy ground. Finally, the voice told him it was the

God of his forefathers Abraham, Isaac, and Jacob. "And Moses hid his face, for he was afraid to look upon God." God told Moses that he knew about the suffering of the Israelites who lived in captivity in Egypt, and he had "come down to deliver them" and lead the Israelites into a beautiful, wide land in which milk and honey flowed.

Moses talks to God.

So far, so good, one assumes. The good Lord ordered a murderer to lead the Israelites out of Egypt, but with God everything has a reason. He sent Moses to Pharaoh to demand the release of his countrymen, and when the latter refused, he subjected Egypt to various plagues.

> *"And I am sure that the king of Egypt will not let you go, no, not by a mighty hand. And I will stretch out my hand and smite Egypt with all my wonders." (Exodus 3:19ff)*

Before the plaguing began, however, God gave an order to steal from the Egyptians. The Israelites were not to leave empty-handed but should borrow diverse pieces of jewelry and clothing, in order to "spoil the Egyptians" (Exodus 3:22 and 12:35–37). This is exactly what is said in the Bible and doesn't correspond at all with the commandment that God later gave to his people: "Thou shalt not steal or covet they neighbor's property." This also shows one of the reasons why Pharaoh did not immediately allow the Israelites to go.

During the further course of the story, Aaron played the second role in these events. Who was Aaron? The *Jewish Encyclopedia* has the answer: Aaron was the oldest son of the Hebrew Amram of the tribe of Levi.[15] Moses, his second son, was three years younger, and their mutual sister, Miriam, was a few years older. Aaron, great-grandson of High Priest Levi, followed his priestly calling within his tribe. While Moses was brought up at the Egyptian royal court, Aaron lived with relatives in the eastern borderlands of Egypt and was known as an outstanding orator. When Moses received God's command to lead the Israelites out of Egyptian captivity, he asked his brother Aaron for help. The fact was that Moses was not at all a good speaker; he required an official spokesman who would present Pharaoh with Israel's demands. During the years that followed, through the Exodus, Aaron advanced to become Moses's deputy and he became High Priest; he enjoyed the special protection of the "Lord in the pillar of cloud." Whenever problems appeared, which required technologically gifted understanding, Aaron was on the spot. He was known as a magician who could conjure up processes that looked like miracles to the masses. Once, as we read in Exodus, Aaron threw his staff to the ground in front of Pharaoh, and the staff was immediately transformed into a living serpent. When the court magician tried to duplicate the trick, Aaron's serpent devoured all the other serpents (Exodus 7:10–12). The same magic staff was used to turn Egypt's waters into a stinking red flood and to create plagues of slimy frogs and troublesome mosquitoes throughout Pharaoh's kingdom.

Moses's and Aaron's appearances at Pharaoh's court were indeed quite spectacular. Apart from the Bible, the *Legends of the Jews* tell us that Moses and Aaron had been afraid of the meeting with Pharaoh. Suddenly, the angel Gabriel had appeared to them and had led the two brothers—right through all the guards—into the palace. Even though the guards were severely punished for their laxness, the same mysterious process happened again at their next visit. Moses and Aaron managed to appear without mishap before the throne of Pharaoh. To be honest, they must have impressed the proud ruler of Egypt quite considerably, as they "resembled angels, their outer appearance reflected and shone like the Sun, the pupils of their eyes were like the brilliance of the morning star, their beards were like young palm fronds, and when they spoke, licking flames came from their mouths."[16] Indeed, it was a most amazing stage-managed happening.

It all turned out as it was written. Moses, supported by his brother Aaron and the magical tricks of his God, triumphed over all Pharaoh's intrigues. The good Lord even let darkness fall on Egypt and mysteriously killed all the firstborn children of the Egyptians. At last, Pharaoh gave up and let the Israelites go. And what did they do?

They constantly complained about and harangued Moses, Aaron, and their new God. Why would they do this? Hadn't God performed unbelievable miracles before their eyes? Did the Israelites still not trust this magic?

According to the Bible, the great trek included 600,000 people "besides children." A large number of foreigners also went with them: "A mixed multitude also went with them; and flocks and herds, even very much cattle" (Exodus 12:37–38). Even if the figure of 600,000 may be considerably exaggerated, or may originate with later writers, the trek had to have been tightly organized. So that this huge mass of people should not wander around aimlessly, "The Lord went before them by day in a pillar of a cloud; and by night in a pillar of fire, to give them light" (Exodus 13:21). In the meantime, the Egyptians had discovered they had been robbed by the Israelites, and Pharaoh sent his armies against the Israelites. The next miracle was now due. "And the angel of God, which went before the camp of Israel, removed and went behind them; and the pillar of the cloud went before their face, and stood behind them." Finally, the Israelite God dried out a strip of sea and then let the entire Egyptian armed forces with all their horses and chariots drown in it, "there remained not so much as one of them" (Exodus 14:28). Now, at last, the Israelites believed in their God and in his servant Moses. This faith was, however, not to last for long.

Why does nobody in our society raise the question about what kind of a God we are dealing with in this story? He favors an ethnic group that does not even believe in him!

The people were made pliable with magic tricks, and it did not seem to matter that the opposition defend themselves when they are robbed. The firstborn of the Egyptians were killed, among them thousands of innocent children. A peculiar column, which sometimes appeared as a brightly shining cloud and then as a frightening pillar of flame, placed itself at the head of this unbelieving procession, and an Egyptian army was drowned without one soldier having drawn his sword. And we should not overlook the fact that the column of fire *deliberately* led the Egyptian army to its doom.

Certainly, with God, nothing is impossible, and he may do what he likes with his creations, but then he ought to be a model for humans and not give his "likenesses" commandments that he does not himself follow. Moreover, the whole business with the plagues that came over Egypt appears to me either to be fictitious or unworthy of the omnipresent creator of the universe. The Koran, the holy writ of Muslims, declares quite laconically, "If he [Allah] decides a thing, he only need say: so be it—and it is so" (Sura 2, verse 117). I see this the same way.

One might assume that after all those wonders and miracles with which God demonstrated his power to the Egyptians as well as to the Israelites, peace would have finally reigned and everyone would have realized who was boss. But this was not the case. Israel's children carried on moaning and murmuring against their God (Exodus 15:24 or 16:2). They were not at all convinced that they were dealing with an almighty being. Even the Lord seemed to realize this, so he decided to show himself to the stubborn people:

And it came to pass, as Aaron spoke unto the whole congregation of the children of Israel, that they looked towards the wilderness, and, behold, the glory of the Lord appeared in the cloud. (Exodus 16:10)

Logically, humans and animals require water and food in the desert. The Lord provided both. He caused springs to bubble up, and in the evening, great flocks of quails fell to the ground above the trek. And every morning, "there lay a small round thing, as small as the hoar frost on the ground." The Israelites did not know what this was, but Moses, instructed beforehand by God, taught them about it. This stuff was called manna, and it was heavenly bread sent by God. The only annoying thing was that this heavenly bread went off quickly, if it was not processed immediately, and it melted like butter in the heat (Exodus 16:20–21). Now, what is manna?

The scholarly disputes about this have lasted for centuries. Generally, it is assumed that manna was the secretion of the scale insect *Coccus manniparus,* which lives off the tamarisk *Tamarix mannifera.* The plant juices of the tamarisk are rich in carbohydrates, and whatever is not absorbed by the insects is secreted in the form of transparent drops that solidify into small white globules in the air. These globules contain fructose and small amounts of pectin (as used for preparing jams). This substance is collected by ants and deposited in their anthills. Bedouins still use this type of manna as a substitute for honey to this day. They call it *man.*

Although there is some similarity between the described substance and the biblical manna, the former seems to lack some of the characteristic features of the food made famous by Moses. *Man* contains no protein, whereas manna in Exodus is described by Moses as "bread" and a staple nourishment. Also, *man* is found for only a few months and in such small quantities that a people wandering in the desert would never have been able to find enough of it. Others think that manna corresponds to the lichen species *Aspicilia esculenta* (manna lichen). But this lichen thrives in tundra landscapes and Alpine meadows, and is hardly found in the desert. Yet manna is supposed to have been a daily, freshly available nourishment.

A third solution to the manna problem was published in the journal *New Scientist* in the spring of 1976.[17] The British authors George Sassoon and Rodney Dale later published their research as a book.[18] The solution suggested by these two Englishmen is so fascinating, and also convincing, that I should like to give a brief account of the story.

Among the edifying and puzzling texts of the ancient Jews are not only the books of the Torah or the *midrashim*, but also of the Kabbala, which are a mixture of ancient secret writings. The Kabbala has become a collective term for the esoteric teachings of Judaism. The term was derived from the Hebrew *QBLH, Qabalah* ("that which is received"). Part of this compendium of Jewish mysticism can be found in the three books of the *Sepher-ha-Zohar* (the Book of Splendor) that is alleged to have been written down by Simon bar Jochai in the second century. The modern versions of the Kabbala were transcribed from ancient texts by the Spanish Jew Moses Ben Shemtob de Leon (thirteenth century). The Latin *Kabbala Denudata* (1644) and the English version *The Kabbala Unveiled* (1892) originate from other sources, mainly from the Aramaic *Cremona Codes* (1558). In the *Zohar* Book of the Kabbala (subdivision *Hadra Zuta Odisha*), about fifty pages are dedicated to the ark of the covenant, which Moses had to build according to God's instructions. The manner of giving the orders in the *Zohar* is more or less identical with the narrative in Exodus, chapter 25, verses 10 ff. But then things become rather strange. In the *Zohar*, Moses had to build not only an ark but also a thing or being with the peculiar name of "Ancient of Days." Both the ark and the "Ancient of Days" were placed in the tent or sacred enclosure and were taken by the Israelites on the long trek. The setting up and dismantling of these objects were carried out by a specially trained priesthood: the Levites. What does the *Zohar* say about this "Ancient of Days"? Here follows a short, bewildering section (from verse 51 of the *Hadra Zuta Odisha*):

> *The upper skull is white. Inside it there is neither beginning nor ending. The hollow thing for its juices is extended and intended for the flowing . . . From this hollow thing for the juices of the white skull, dew falls daily into the small-faced thing. . . . And its head is filled, and from the small-faced thing it falls onto a field of apples [or bellows]. And the entire field of apples flows with this dew. The Ancient of Days is mysterious and hidden. And the superior wisdom is hidden in the skull, which was found [or viewed]. And from that one to this one, the Ancient was never opened . . . And there is not a son of Man who knows this thing. [It is not comprehensible to anyone] . . . Three heads are hollow. This is in one and this above another . . . And all its hairs and its cords are hidden and smooth inside a container. And the neck cannot be seen entirely . . . There is a pathway, which flows into the parting of the hairs, from the brain . . .*

And the text goes on in this fashion for many pages. One gets the impression of a stream of child-like babble. But linguist George Sassoon was able to make sense of this muddle. Sassoon could read Aramaic and was able to find a meaning for many of the incomprehensible terms used. What could it be, this "Ancient of Days" with several heads, cords, dew, special brains, and light sources in its belly? According to the description in the book of *Zohar,* this Ancient of Days consisted of male and female parts. These two parts could be taken apart and cleaned by the Levite priests. Peculiar. How could something divine be taken apart and put together again? George Sassoon weeded out some of the margin notes and soon noticed that this was not about a living being but about a machine. This apparatus produced something that was available fresh and daily. Could it have been manna?

The book of *Zohar,* which includes the story of the manna machine.

This was the moment when Sassoon required the help of a biologist. Rodney Dale was a biologist and also someone who was able to translate confusing biological processes into technological terms. Finally, Martin Riches, a scientific illustrator, joined the team, and soon the Ancient of Days was revealed as a biochemical machine.

The manna machine, according to Dale and Sassoon.

The bewildering Kabbala text results in an astonishing revelation: The Ancient of Days had two skulls, one above the other; both were contained within an outer skull. The upper skull contained the upper brain, in which dew was distilled. The lower skull contained the divine oil. The Ancient had four eyes, one of which shone very brightly from inside; the other three shone more faintly, from left to right, black, yellow, and red. As is proper for an Ancient, it had a voluminous beard in thirteen different variations. Many hairs grew out of its face and then back again at the bottom of its face. These hairs were soft, and the holy oil ran through them.

Then there was a "small skull" (the small-faced one), in which fire developed on one side and air on the other. Some kind of oil flowed from the upper skull into the lower skull, and there changed color from white to red. Something "honey-like" flowed through the "cords," down into a testicle. When one testicle was full, the overflow of honey flowed into a second testicle. The left testicle was emptied daily via the "penis," then cleaned; the right testicle filled up more on a daily basis and was emptied only on the Sabbath, then cleaned the following day. But what was this all about?

The upper part of the Ancient of Days was simply a distilling device with a corrugated, cooling surface, over which air could pass and water was condensed. The "cords" were conducting lines, which allowed water to flow into a container with a strong source of light. This light irradiated a culture of algae—possibly of the *Chlorella* type. There are dozens of *Chlorella* species, whose equilibrium between protein, carbohydrates, and fats can be altered according to its conditions for growth. The algae culture circulated within a system of pipes that enabled an exchange of oxygen and carbon dioxide with the atmosphere and allowed excess heat to escape. The *Chlorella* slime was conducted into another container, where it was treated in a way that partially hydrolyzed the starch into maltose, which was then lightly heated to produce the taste of honey wafers. Just as it is described in Exodus:

> *And it was like coriander seed, white; and the taste of it was like wafers made with honey. (Exodus 16:31)*

The dried product was then conducted into two vessels (the "testicles"). One of these served the daily requirements; the other one filled up gradually to provide a store for the Sabbath. The apparatus did not work during the weekly Sabbath break and was maintained so that it was ready to work again from Sunday onwards.

This manna was a basic nourishment that contained protein, comparable with flour, and which could be made into different breads or flat pancake-like foods in the hot desert sand. It was manufactured by means of a wondrous, highly technological device. The water collected in the form of dew during the night was mixed with small parts of the *Chlorella* algae. When this species of algae is irradiated, it can multiply at an unbelievable rate within twenty-four hours. The machine had to deliver one *omer* per day, per family. (One *omer* was a Hebrew volume measure and was equivalent to about three liters.) At this time, there were only about 600 families left to supply, so the output of the manna machine should have been about 1.5 cubic meters per day. So what became of this miraculous manna machine?

The priests of the Levites were the only ones who knew how to maintain and clean the apparatus. Moses's brother, Aaron, was the chief of the Levites and had received his instructions directly from the Lord. Once the machine was no longer being maintained properly, no heavenly food was dispensed. The prophet Joshua bemoaned this fact: "And the manna ceased on the morrow after they had eaten of the corn of the old land" (Joshua 5:12). After the fall of Jericho, the apparatus was stored in a place called Shiloh (1 Samuel 4:3). Later, the Philistines captured the manna machine together with the ark of the covenant. According to Sassoon and Dale, the ark was no less than a generator (supplying the energy) for the manna machine. It is a fact that the Ancient of Days and the ark were always placed side by side in the holy tent (1 Samuel 6–8). It is not surprising that, when it was not maintained correctly, the ark often caused fatal accidents, even among the trained Levite specialists (1 Samuel 5:11–12 or 2 Samuel 6:3–7). The Philistines, on the other hand, who had captured the devices, had no idea how to work the ark and the manna machine. Many of them died of terrible diseases because they had been too close to the technological monster. Full of fear, the Philistines sent this loot back to Israel without making any demands. King Solomon (the Wise) had a special shrine built in the temple to house the ark and the manna machine. By this time, none of these devices were functioning any more, and neither Solomon nor David was able to get the magic processes to work again. In the end, a son of Solomon stole parts of the machine and took them to his mother, the Queen of Sheba. This is detailed in the Book of Ethiopian Kings.[19]

The entry of the ark of the covenant into Jerusalem.

And what is the status today? The remains are alleged to lie deep in the ground under the cathedral of Mary in the Ethiopian city of Axum.

It would be easy just to smile at this reconstruction of a manna machine in the Kabbala, but it is still a brilliant idea, and scientifically beautifully illustrated. Many parts of the puzzle cannot be found in the Bible, even though the "Word of God" provides some clues that should make us think. Who has noticed, for example, that the transportation of the ark required two carts? Read this in 2 Samuel, chapter 6, verse 3.

> And they set the ark of God upon a new cart . . . and Uzzah and
> Ahio, the sons of Abinadab, drove the new cart.

This same Uzzah later died—"God smote him there for his error"—when he touched the ark during transport and it was shaken by the oxen. Divine punishment? What for?

Only because he had tried to steady the ark to prevent it overturning?

There are many puzzles about the ark of the covenant, even among the theologians. First of all, Moses had to build a curious box or casket according to the Lord's exact instructions (Exodus 25:10). These instructions would not have been only verbal, as the good Lord was in possession of an original:

And look that thou make them after their pattern, which was shewed thee in the mount. (Exodus 25:40)

The purpose of this strange box is also disputed. Theologian Rainer Schmitt thinks the ark "is a container for a holy stone."[20] This is contradicted by famous theologian Martin Dibelius, who thinks we are dealing with a "portable, empty throne of God, or a wheeled vehicle of God on which stood or sat the Godhead."[21] Theologian R. Vatke sees it differently again. He maintains there was "nothing inside the ark, because God lived inside it."[22] Harry Torczyner thinks the tablets with the commandments were transported in the ark.[23] This was questioned again by Martin Dibelius. There are even passages in the Bible that tell us of the ark: "And the ark of the covenant of the Lord went before them in the three days' journey, to search out a resting place for them" (Numbers 10:33). Did the Lord not know in advance where the Israelites ought to camp? And so on! The subject is endless. Whoever takes the trouble to dip into Otto Eissfeldt's 1,000-page work on theology will soon have some inkling about this subject.[24]

The ark was a lethally dangerous object. This is not just something we can read about in the Bible; the Torah scholars are also aware of this. Philosopher and mathematician

Lazarus Bendavid (1762–1832), former head of a Jewish school, wrote nearly 200 years ago:

> [T]he holy hut at Moses's time must have contained a fairly complete device incorporating electrical instruments. According to the talmudists, entering the Holy of Holies was always tantamount to being in mortal danger. The High Priest always performed this duty with a certain degree of fear and counted himself lucky when he emerged again safely.[25]

But what kind of God—and this is really the cardinal question in this chapter—would have his top secret servants (Moses and Aaron) build him a special box, for which there was already an original? What God would have them take apart an "Ancient of Days" and clean it? What God would have them transport an extremely dangerous apparatus that is proven to have led to several deaths? Would an omnipresent Spirit of the Universe really require such drama? One could object that all this was a matter of interpretation and that God was only interested in getting humans to believe deeply in him. But this is exactly the problem. Are we supposed to believe doggedly in a God surrounded by contradictions and errors of judgment? If this were really God's purpose, every sect would have free rein to believe in their *own* interpretation and their own Bible. Every group is, naturally, of honest intention and convinced that *their* version of the Holy Writ, *their* translation, is the only true one. My own feelings are that it would contradict divine intelligence to allow one's creatures to believe in something they must realize cannot be so. The command "You must believe, even if you see errors" is unintelligent in the deepest sense. The path to so-called salvation can surely not include holding on to misunderstandings and nonsense. The creative spirit of the universe is, above all, timeless and eternal. "It" would know that its intelligent creatures would start looking for new explanations for old contradictions sometime in the future. If indeed "salvation" exists within the divine principle, then it must lie in realization. "Believing is a comfort, thinking an effort" (Ludwig Marcuse, 1894–1971).

The God described in the Old Testament disposes of powers that go far beyond anything humans in those times understood. As we know from our present, a technologically inferior group of people will perceive every advanced weapon as magic. I wrote an earlier book about this.[26] This same goes for the Old Testament. There we have a battle between the Israelites and the Amalekites. Moses sent his warriors into battle under the leadership of Joshua, while he, together with Aaron and Hur, climbed on to a nearby hill. What for?

And it came to pass, when Moses held up his hand, that Israel prevailed, and when he let down his hand, Amalek prevailed. But Moses's hands were heavy; and they took a stone, and put it under him, and he sat thereon; and Aaron and Hur stayed up his hands, the one on the one side, and the other on the other side; and his hands were steady until the going down of the sun. (Exodus 17:11 ff)

The Israelites won the battle, and the good Lord told Moses, he would "utterly put out the remembrance of Amalek under heaven"—in other words, he would wipe them out.

What a situation! Lacking the evidence, we do not know what kind of weapon Moses used from his strategic position on the hill, but it must have been something heavy. His closest confidants had to help hold up his arms. And their enemies were completely wiped out. This is divine?

The absolute climax of meetings between Moses and his God takes place in chapters 19 and 20 of Exodus. First, Moses climbed "up to the top of the mount." The Lord gave Moses the order to tell his people that now they had seen what he had done to the Egyptians and how he had "bare you on eagles" wings, and brought you unto myself. Because of this, henceforth, the people should listen only to his voice and keep his covenant. "Then ye shall be a peculiar treasure unto me above all people: for all the earth is mine." There seems no point in asking why the creative spirit of the universe required a "possession." As the indecisive people still wavered, the Lord decided, "Lo, I will come to thee in a thick cloud, that the people may hear when I speak with thee, and believe thee forever." Finally, the Lord declared that he would come down onto Mount Sinai in front of the whole people, the day after next. This did not, however, appear to have been quite that feasible, as Moses had first to draw a boundary around the mountain:

> And thou shalt set bounds unto the people round about, saying, Take heed to yourselves, that ye go not up into the mount, or touch the border of it; whosoever toucheth the mount shall be surely put to death; There shall not an hand touch it, but he shall surely be stoned, or shot through; whether it be beast or man, it shall not live. (Exodus 19:12)

A few verses on, there are additional instructions:

> [C]harge the people, lest they break through unto the Lord to gaze, and many of them perish. (Exodus 19:21)

This ban applied equally to the priests, "lest the Lord break forth upon them."

Even if further passages were required to show that Moses was not speaking to the omnipresent spirit of the universe but to something quite different, these sentences provide the evidence. Why can this incomparable and unique God not protect them himself? And indeed, what from? Why does he require a barrier around the mountain?

Why the dreadful warnings of death? The Lord should have known that these beings created "in his image" were curious. If, for whatever reasons, he did not wish these humans or animals to come near him, why could he not have put up a protective shield around the mountain? Was he not capable of doing it? Naturally, theologians see this differently. Of course, they have had thousands of years to come up with something complicated to explain the banal. The good Lord wanted to draw a line between the profane and the holy, between the ordinary and the extraordinary. The profane ought to lie outside a holy area, and later on, outside the temple. Inside the holy area is the dwelling place of the incomprehensible, the secret, which humans may not approach, and which they would not be able to understand anyway. The holy area or enclosure, according to the *Brockhaus* dictionary, contains the infinitely superior, the ungraspable, the otherwordly power.[27]

That is what it must be. Holy boundaries, places of awe, have existed in all cultures and religions from the most distant past to the present. But what are the origins of this thinking? In Exodus, the Lord defines the boundaries around the mountain. Would it have not been sufficient to punish those humans (and animals) who crossed the line with a beating? Was it not possible to prevent them, by means of an insurmountable barrier, from straying into the holy area? Evidently, this was not possible in Exodus. Why? Because the Lord came down upon the mountain. And how!

> *And mount Sinai was altogether on a smoke, because the Lord descended upon it in fire: and the smoke thereof ascended as the smoke of a furnace, and the whole mount quaked greatly . . . And the Lord came down upon the mount Sinai, on the top of the mount . . . (Exodus 19:18 ff)*

> *And it came to pass on the third day in the morning, that there were thunders and lightnings, and a thick cloud upon the mount, and the voice of the trumpet exceeding loud; so that all the people that was in the camp trembled. (Exodus 19:16)*

The Lord descends on the holy mountain.

And who would have not trembled at this demonstration? Separating off a holy area seemed almost superfluous. Now at last, the obstinate people appeared to have comprehended that the God of Israel disposed of mighty powers, that he was the true God, and that Moses's word was absolute law. This insight did not last for long. Moses walked into the cloud "in which was God" to receive the ten commandments from him. We have all had to learn these commandments at some time in our R.E. lessons. They are wonderful rules for living together that would be sensible in the entire universe for all intelligent forms of life. And the only basis for differing interpretations could be found in the first two commandments. The Lord commanded:

Thou shalt have no other gods before me. (Exodus 20:3)

Why? Were there any other gods? Assuredly, the different peoples in that time without history worshipped various nature gods like the Sun, the Moon, the stars, and so on. And they also prayed to homemade idols. But gods, "those who descended from above" (the Hebrew *elohim*)? Who, apart from the God of the Israelites, had descended?

The most diverse gods worshipped by "other peoples" are described in 2 Kings, chapters 17–21. Deuteronomy abounds with the brutal destruction of those peoples who had worshipped "other gods." The God of the Old Testament books brooked no rivals. And he specifically commanded not to make any images of him:

Thou shalt not make unto thee any graven image, or any likeness of any thing that is in heaven above, or that is in the earth beneath, or that is in the water under the earth. (Exodus 20:4)

That means not even an image of God himself. That would have been impossible anyway, because the people never caught sight of this jealous God. Nevertheless, they were allowed to marvel, several times, at "the splendor of the Lord," a "something" that shone, made rushing sounds and noises, churned up the sand and was, in addition, extremely dangerous. But the God of the Old Testament desired humans not to make an image of it. Why? Would it not have served the divine mysticism if humans had illustrated this mysterious thing? Did the Lord fear that humans of the distant future might identify such illustrations as something technological?

We do not know because, in the end, everything became a question of interpretation, or just a view from a different period of time. Today, the things described in the Old Testament provide quite a clear idea of what must have been going on. But this too must have been obvious to an omnipresent God with all his timeless understanding. One just cannot get past all this, if we concede timelessness as an attribute of the nature of God.

The descent of the splendor of the Lord is supposed to have taken place on Mount Sinai, or the Jebel Musa (Moses mount). The mountain is said to have smoked "like a furnace." Can such statements be verified? Should one not be able to find carbonized or even molten rocks around the Jebel Musa? The "whole mount quaked greatly," we are told. That should have left behind some traces. Moreover, the landing was described as dangerous, and nobody was allowed to step over the holy boundary. Would it be possible to measure this uncanny thing with modern instruments?

In principle, it should be possible, but nobody bothers. Jebel Musa lies in the Sinai peninsula, in present-day Egypt, and is often visited by tourists. The mountain itself resembles a dried-up, deeply fissured stone desert. An ordinary Geiger counter will at best provide vague measurements about radioactivity. But then, who says the danger was of a radioactive nature? Nobody knows in what year the Lord is supposed to have descended upon the mountain. Theologians state that we know the dates of Moses, and the Old Testament chronology was clearly set. Unfortunately, this is not true. The chronology of the Old Testament is full of contradictions and is based on nothing but pious wishful thinking. To find evidence of inconsistencies at the mountain of Moses, one would need to know the period in which the events took place, then employ quite different instruments of measurement than simple Geiger counters. Beyond this, the scholars are not even agreed on whether the good Lord actually "descended" on Jebel Musa. Italian archaeologist Dr. Emmanuel Anati thinks the dramatic event really happened on the mountain called Har Karkom in present-day southern Israel. A different view is taken by British archaeologist Lawrence Kyle, who has identified present-day Hallat-al-Bedr in Saudi Arabia as the holy mountain. Dr. Kamal S. Salibi, in an exciting and expertly researched book, demonstrates that the entire Moses story could never have taken place on the Sinai peninsula at all but occurred in Saudi Arabia.[28] How, then, did one arrive at all this?

Everyone knows that the Israelites crossed the Jordan several times during their wanderings. We all think that the little Jordan River is meant. In reality, however, the Jordan is a chain of mountains in the Saudi Arabian province of Asir. Everyone knows that Moses liberated his people from slavery in Egypt. In the end, the Lord destroyed the Egyptian army.

The curious thing is that neither ancient Egyptian inscriptions nor any traditions show up any trace of Israelite captives, not to speak of hints of an exodus or the destruction of an Egyptian army. Not even Greek historian Herodotus, who spent quite some time in Egypt and noted all kinds of minutiae and every date of Egyptian history, learned anything about Israel, about a Hebrew tribe in Egyptian captivity, about an exodus of a people from Egypt, let alone a "divine" destruction of the Egyptian army.

We have all read about the trumpets of Jericho, which brought down the walls of the ancient city. Archaeologists have long known without doubt that the event narrated by the prophet Joshua could never have occurred in the Jericho of present-day Palestine, on evidence of dating alone. Theologians who believe in the Bible have twisted things to fit the story in the Old Testament and make it believable. Whenever a ruin, an inscription, a water hole, a potsherd, or a crumbling scrap of fabric was found in Palestine, one was immediately ready to convert every little detail into alleged proof for the truth of the Bible. What is really going on here was investigated in a critical article in *Der Spiegel* about three works on Bible archaeology: "All three volumes were full of archaeological pseudo-revelations."[29] Very little in the Exodus book fits the Sinai peninsula, but a lot, on the other hand, does fit with Saudi Arabia—even the names of the mountains and the tombs.

One hundred and thirty kilometers south of the town of Taif (Saudi Arabia, Asir province) lies the Jebel Ibrahim (2,595 meters), the mountain of Abraham. A further 150 kilometers south of this, one comes across Solomon's original country: Al Suleiman. On the summit of Jebel Shada lie the remains of an altar from the Stone Age with indecipherable inscriptions: *Musalla Ibrahim*—Abraham's place of prayer. Southeast of Abha (Asir) is the 2,100-meter Jebel Harun, Aaron's mountain. Many founding fathers and prophets of the Old Testament lie buried in the mountains of Saudi Arabia and the bordering Yemen. Up until 1950, tourists were still being taken to the tombs of Cain and Abel on the Jebel Hadid. The tomb of the patriarch Job lies on the middle peak of the Jebel Hesha in North Yemen, and the vault of the prophet Hud is still counted among the most important Arab holy shrines. It lies north of Tarim in the Hadhramaut Mountains. This is all very bewildering and would, on the face of it, not be so important if so many generations of people had not been brainwashed into believing to this day that the Old Testament events had taken place in Sinai and Palestine. So there are a number of prophets' tombs in modern Israel and Palestine, although these gentlemen, even according to the Bible, could never have been buried there. Moses is just one example. In Deuteronomy, chapter 34, the Lord says this was the land that he had sworn to give Abraham, Isaac, and Jacob, "but thou shalt not go over thither . . . and Moses the servant of the Lord died there in the land of Moab . . . but no man knoweth of his sepulchre unto this day."

So why do more than 100,000 people yearly make a pilgrimage to the tomb of Moses in Palestine? Once, Sultan Saladin dreamed that Allah had brought the mortal remains of Moses from an unknown tomb to Palestine. This dream was sufficient to erect a shrine with a tomb to Moses. In 1265, Sultan Baibars had a mosque erected over the tomb, and in the fifteenth century the Mamelukes built a splendid hostel with 400 rooms beside it. Today, the tomb of Moses is one of the great pilgrimage places of Islam—only, Moses is not buried there. This is the state of affairs, with the descriptions in the Old Testament contradicting hard reality.

The location of Aaron's tomb is also the subject of these games of confusion. Jebel Harun with Aaron's tomb lies 2,100 meters up, southeast of Abha (Saudi Arabia, near the provincial town of Asir). A second burial place can be found on the top of a mountain called Ohod near Medina.[30] A third tomb in Moseroth in present-day Israel, and Aaron's fourth resting place, is on top of a mountain near the Jordanian city of Petra. I visited this tomb myself many years ago.[31] According to the Bible, Aaron died on the top of Mount Hor:

> And the children of Israel, even the whole congregation, journeyed from Kades, and came unto mount Hor. And the Lord spake unto Moses and Aaron in mount Hor, by the coast of the land of Edom, saying Aaron shall be gathered unto his people: for he shall not enter into the land which I have given unto the children of Israel, because ye rebelled against my word at the water of Meribah. Take Aaron and Eleazar his son, and bring them up unto mount Hor: And strip Aaron of his garments, and put them on Eleazar, his son: and Aaron shall be gathered unto his people, and shall die there. And Moses did as the Lord commanded: and they went up into mount Hor in the sight of all the congregation. And Moses stripped Aaron of his garments, and put them upon Eleazar his son; and Aaron died there in the top of the mount: and Moses and Eleazar came down from the mount. And when all the congregation saw that Aaron was dead, they mourned for Aaron thirty days, even all the house of Israel. (Numbers 20:22 ff)

In the *Legends of the Jews*,[32] there is a variation about Aaron's death. On Mount Hor, a cave suddenly opened up and Moses invited his brother to enter. Then Moses said it was a silly idea to enter a dirty cave with priest's clothing, so Aaron took off his clothes. Moses immediately handed them to Eleazar, and Aaron understood that this was to be his place of death. As Aaron stood naked in front of the cave, eight items of divine clothing floated by and covered Aaron's nakedness. Everything is possible in legends. In this one, Aaron's death bed flew through the air, and Aaron died by a kiss of God. Islam sees all this slightly differently again:

> *Mousa and Haroun [Moses and Aaron] once found a cave from which light issued forth. They went in and found a golden throne with the inscription: Intended for someone whom it fits. As Mousa thought it was too small for him, Haroun sat on it. At once, the angel of death appeared and received his soul. He was 127 years old.*[33]

It makes little sense to go searching for the tombs of the venerable patriarchs and biblical prophets in the Holy Land. They do exist, but the revered great men of the Bible are not inside them. Another example, symptomatic for the chaos created by Muslims, people who believe in the Bible and the Torah, is the tomb of the legendary Abraham. His sphere of activity was the place called Mambre, 2 kilometers north of the town of Hebron in present-day Israel. This hilly region is the classical ground of all the stories about Abraham, and unbelievable things are alleged to have occurred here thousands of years ago. According to the Bible, Abraham had settled here with his herds and tents and had erected an altar to God. From there, he chased after the

Babylonian warriors with 318 of his servants to liberate Lot and his family. Mambre was even the location of the memorable meeting between God and Abraham, for here it was that the Lord promised Abraham that his descendants would be as numerous as the stars in heaven. Finally, it was in Mambre that God commanded ritual circumcision. Abraham, who at ninety-nine years old was beyond good or evil, set the example and allowed his foreskin to be cut off—together with that of his thirteen-year-old son, Ishmael.

They must have been exciting times, long, long ago in Mambre. One day, Abraham was sitting in front of his tent, when three strangers turned up. Hospitable as the founding father was, he had a young calf slaughtered and generously entertained his guests with food. His son [Ishmael] did not fail to notice that the strangers were "no descendants of the nature of Earth dwellers."[34] In the Testament of Abraham, an old Jewish tradition, the visitors are termed "heavenly men," who came down from heaven and then went back there.

Now, the Bible tells us that Abraham had bought a plot of land with a cave "opposite Mambre" for 400 Lot silver (Genesis 23:9 ff). There he had himself and his wife Sarah buried. His son Isaac with his wife Rebekah and his grandson Jacob with his wives Lea and Rachel should have been buried in this vault too, of course.

But nothing is as simple as that. In Deuteronomy, chapter 34, the Lord says this was the country that he had promised Abraham, Isaac, and Jacob, but he, Moses, should not go thither.

Why does nobody question this nonsense? How can the Lord promise Abraham land that his descendants would obtain in the future if the same Abraham is already in this land—Mambre—and has been for ages?

And what is this business with Abraham's family vault? In the center of the city of Hebron today we see the huge, rectangular Haram-al-Ibrahimi Mosque, a wonderful holy place for Muslims, Jews, and Christians. Crypts are situated on both sides of the middle section, beneath which Isaac's and Rebekah's graves are said to lie. Leaf-green cloths embroidered with Arabic script can be seen through the brass grids. The words tell us: "This is the tomb of the prophet Abraham. May he rest in peace." Four small white columns support a marble super-structure like a canopy, which is covered with a dark wooden plate. Underneath, sixty-eight steep steps are said to lead down to the site of Abraham's grave. This mosque is now one of the holiest sites of Islam. But Abraham's grave is inaccessible. At the time of the crusades (eleventh to thirteenth centuries), an Islamic mosque stood on this spot. What may have stood there even earlier is not known. The crusaders turned the mosque into a Christian monastery. Hebron was called Saint Abraham's City.

One day, a praying monk felt a draft coming from a corner. He pursued the source of this draft, together with his monastic brothers. The venerable gentlemen tapped the walls and discovered a spot that sounded hollow. In the end, they removed a stone slab and uncovered a cavern. Up to this point, the monks knew only from Arabic traditions that their monastery had been built above the Machpela Cave, Abraham's vault. They broke through the wall and found behind it a small, circular room. But there was no sign of a tomb.

One of these pious searchers could not accept the bitter disappointment. He continued to tap the walls and discovered a wedge-shaped stone that had been inserted into it. The stone was pulled out with great effort, and lo and behold, an entire wall crumbled. In the flickering light of torches, the monks discovered bleached bones on the floor and, in a niche, fifteen urns that contained rattling bones. No objects of any kind had been deposited with the burials—no inscriptions, no fabric, nothing that pointed to Abraham or his family. Hymns were sung in praise of the Lord, and later some of the bones were sold as relics of Abraham. "Since that time, nobody has been inside the Machpela Cave," states Danish research traveler Arne Falk-Ronne, who was following Abraham's trail.[35]

Today, it is not possible to check whether the discovery of the tomb happened in exactly that way, and whether the monks and crusaders really did find something that pointed to Abraham. It is generally known that many items were transferred from the Holy Land into European monasteries and to the Vatican at the time of the Crusades. The Muslims who today guard the Mosque of Abraham refuse to enter Abraham's tomb, as Allah would punish with blindness anyone who would dare to violate the resting place of the founding father. Orthodox Jews likewise prevent any kind of archaeological research with such arguments. The time is not ripe to pursue these riddles without prejudice. It might just be that the spade would suddenly bring surprises to the light of day that would turn out to be very uncomfortable. His descendants would not have allowed a figure such as Abraham to disappear quietly into some vault. He was, after all, the progenitor, the founding father of all the generations that followed, one of those who had spoken with God and his servants. Accordingly, reverence for him would have been very deep indeed. If Abraham's sons had really buried him in the Machpela Cave, this spot would have become a place of pilgrimage for all subsequent generations. This would have been even more the case, as another five persons worthy of veneration were laid to rest with him, figures revered by three world religions. Nothing of all of this is to be seen in Hebron. So where could Abraham have been buried then, and why is his grave unknown?

Professor Kamal Salibi demonstrates that both Mambre as well as the Machpela Cave can be found in the Saudi Arabian province of Asir. The grove in which Abraham settled "consists of small acacias and tamarisk stands in the vicinity of Namira and Hirban, in the hinterland of Qunfudha."[36] In the same hilly country, near a little place called Maqfala *(mqflh)*, is the double cave called Machpelah *(mkplh)*. So why did this important site never become an important place of pilgrimage?

The Israelites were beaten by the Babylonians and carried off into captivity, scattered in all directions. The Babylonians had quite different gods. They did not know Abraham, who meant nothing to them, and they had a different religion. Abraham's descendants—David, Solomon, and so on—settled in what is now present-day Israel, and no tomb of Abraham existed there. If one takes the Bible literally, Abraham begat (among many other children) Isaac, the same one who was nearly sacrificed by Abraham, who was following God's orders. This sacrifice was prevented by the intervention of an angel. Isaac then begat his twin sons

Esau and Jacob. Esau was the oldest son and the first in line to inherit. Jacob did not care and contrived to rob his brother of his firstborn rights. When the aged Isaac became blind, and according to tradition was ready to bless and acknowledge his firstborn son, his wife Rebekah and the second-born son deceived him. The old man promptly blessed Jacob instead of Isaac (Genesis 27). It was then quite understandable that Esau, who had been cheated out of his inheritance, no longer wanted anything to do with his family. A Phoenician legend tells that Esau was a direct descendant of the race of gods known as the Titans, those who had "still fought with the celestial powers."[37] The Bible has nothing to say about Esau's death, let alone about where he was buried. Not so the pseudo-epigraphs of the Old Testament. *Pseudo-epigraphs* is the name given to texts that are not included in the Bible but still belong to the group of biblical history. Among these is the "testament of Judah, the fourth son of Jacob and Lea." The text is rendered in the first person singular.[38] Judah gives an account of his birth, his youth, and his battles. One reads with astonishment how Judah fought with the giant Achor, who "launched bolts to the front and back of his horse." Then, the person narrating the story tells us that his father Jacob had lived together in peace with Esau for eighteen years. Not until then did Esau demand his inheritance, and he rose up against Jacob with a mighty people. Esau died during the battle and was buried in the mountains of Seir, wherever they might be, certainly not in the Holy Land. But there, in an Arab village north of Hebron, tourists are led into the Mosque of Si'ir, under which, allegedly, lies the grave of Esau. It was a confusing time, and the stories about it have been taken for granted.

The Bible is only one of many sources about this prehistoric epoch. If the Bible were historical, the geographical places, the neighboring regions, and the tombs of these hero figures should be found in the right places. They are not. Abraham, just like all the other patriarchs, is not to be found where he should be.

According to the Jewish traditions, there is supposed to have been a city called Salem (*slm*) during Abraham's time. This Salem cannot, however, be identical with the later Jerusalem, as Jerusalem was founded by Solomon—or so we believe. We have already heard that Abraham enjoyed God's special protection from birth and that God "loved him specially." This mysterious city of Salem was ruled by a king called Melchizedek, who was not the product of an ordinary human conception, as God himself is said to have planted his seed in Sopranima, Melchizedek's mother. (Ancient literature abounds with similar, divine in-vitro conceptions.) This same Melchizedek once met Abraham and "blessed him." It must be obvious that these muddling events around the time of Abraham do not fit into any timeline.

Christian theologians and many leaders of smaller religious communities still look upon the Bible as the Word of God. This lack of judgment is part of a system. We humans are instructed from birth in the faith and are encouraged to reject all foreign influences. Any doubts whatsoever that were put to a community of a particular faith were judged to be—and still are—devilish! Pope Paul IV knew exactly what he was about in 1559—when only a few people were able to read—when he had a list of books compiled called the *Index librorum prohibitorum*, a list of forbidden books. This *Index* was revoked by Pope Paul VI in 1967, but believers to this day are not really meant to devour books that question their faith. My opinion is that for those critical believers who are not inclined to swallow everything but have the courage to raise questions, the Bible alone is sufficient to make one's hair stand on end.

After Moses had received the ten commandments and the whole population had been witness to the impressive sight of God descending upon the mountain, their lack of faith immediately got the upper hand again. The common people in the camp at the foot of the holy mountain became impatient and started fashioning a golden calf out of jewelry and precious metals of all kinds. Then they worshipped this idol. It seems quite unbelievable that even Aaron, Moses's brother, who was after all the High Priest of the Levites, joined in this blasphemy. Understandably, Moses was "angered" at the sight of the golden calf. He smashed the brand new tablets featuring the commandments and, on God's command, ordered that 3,000 people be put to death:

> *Put every man his sword by his side, and go in and out from gate to gate, throughout the camp, and slay every man his brother, and every man his companion, and every man his neighbor. And the children of Levi did according to the word of Moses: and there fell of the people that day about three thousand men. (Exodus 32:27–28)*

The Lord, who once again did not know how the stubborn Israelites would react during Moses's absence, was angry, but he still promised to lead them to the country where milk and honey flowed. He himself, though, did not seem to feel like traveling with them any more, "For I will not go up in the midst of thee; for thou art a stiff-necked people: lest I consume thee in the way" (Exodus 33:3). Nevertheless, he appears to be mollified by jewelry : "Therefore now put off thy ornaments from thee, that I may know what to do unto thee." My kingdom for a plausible explanation as to what God was going to do with the jewelry!

Still, he did provide an angel as his deputy, who drove away the peoples already living in the Promised Land: "And I will send an angel before thee; and I will drive out the Canaanite, the Amorite, and the Hittite, and the Pirizzite, the Hivite, and the Jebusite" (Exodus 33:2). Cool!

Before the journey could continue, Moses set up the holy tent (the tabernacle) outside the camp and called it the "tent of the meeting." Here, we have not just the ark of the covenant together with the "Ancient of Days," but also a strange pillar of cloud placed itself at all times protectively in front of the entrance to the tent whenever Moses and Aaron were inside. The Lord is supposed to have spoken to Moses in the tent, face to face, "as a man speaketh unto his friend." But wait! Exactly the opposite is written in the same chapter 33 of Exodus. While verse 11 assures us that the Lord spoke to Moses, face to face, as a man to his friend, verses 18, 19, and 20 convey a very different impression. There, Moses implores God, "I beseech thee, shew me thy glory." And verse 23, "and when I take mine hand, and thou shalt see my back parts, but my face shall not be seen."

The same rejection is taken for granted in the Gilgamesh epic: "Who looks upon the gods' faces must die."

Would humans perhaps have become infected with alien viruses or bacteria, and were the gods unable to prevent this? Or was it the other way around? Were the gods afraid of becoming

infected by humans? Was this the real reason for the holy enclo-
sures, the temple forecourts and inner holies of holies, into
which only priests were allowed, who had been cleansed several
times and well instructed? God in quarantine? What kind of
God? What kind of gods? In Numbers, we find that conversations between God and his servant are once more conducted
in relative terms. Now God only communicates with Moses by
means of a kind of loudspeaker:

> *And when Moses was gone into the tabernacle of the congrega-
> tion to speak with him, then he heard the voice of one speaking
> unto him from off the mercy seat that was upon the ark of testi-
> mony from between the two cherubims: and he spake unto him.
> (Numbers 7:89)*

It really is a bit much, what is expected of the simple
believer in the way of contradictions. Once again, the people
murmur against their God. This time it is about the boring
menu. Moses had the not-very-sensible idea of asking the
Lord for meat. The Lord promptly organized a strong wind,
which blew a flock of quails across from the sea and had
them plunge to the ground over the Israelites' camp. There
must have been a huge number of them, as the little birds
lay around the camp, "as it were a day's journey on this side,
and as it were, a day's journey on the other side, round about
the camp and as it were two cubits high upon the face of the
earth" (Numbers 11:31). As one would expect, the Israelites
gathered up the quails, to dry them and also to make immedi-
ate meals of them. But "while the flesh was yet between their
teeth, ere it was chewed, the wrath of the Lord was kindled
against the people, and the Lord smote the people with a very

great plague" (Numbers, 11:33). Why did the Lord provide huge quantities of quails, only to punish the hungry people? Were the Israelites perhaps intended, for some reason, only to consume food that was made of the basic substance of manna?

Time and again, the God of the Old Testament drums into his people that he had "separated" the Israelites from all other peoples (Leviticus 20:24). Consequently, the new rules were very different and were to be strictly adhered to. Adultery was to be punishable by death, for both man and woman. The same went for son-in-law and mother-in-law, but even for one's own wife and her mother, if the husband were to "take both to wife." Homosexuals were also immediately condemned to death: "They shall surely be put to death. Their blood shall be upon them." These harsh directives can be found in Leviticus, chapter 20, verses 10 ff. The same unmerciful attitude is to be shown to fortune-tellers: "A man also or woman that hath a familiar spirit, or that is a wizard, shall surely be put to death: they shall stone them with stones: their blood shall be upon them" (Leviticus 20:27). Evidently, the same did not apply to the innumerable tellers of the future who were later called prophets. They were forever having visions, enlightenments, or apparitions without instantly being slaughtered for it. Special rules applied to priests too; today they would be regarded as discrimination. Anyone who was in the slightest way disabled was not allowed to be near the altar. The same went for the blind and the lame, for those with mutilated faces, or for anyone who had "anything superfluous." Woe to anyone who served God and who had a blemish or was injured in an accident: "a man that is brokenfooted or brokenhanded; no man that hath a blemish in his eye, or be scurvy, or scabbed, or has his stones broken" was allowed to approach the Lord (Leviticus 21:17 ff).

Even a bad word against the new God, a quiet curse, was to be punished with death immediately by stoning (Leviticus 24:13). If one did damage to one's neighbor, the same should be done to him, so "breach for breach, eye for eye, tooth for tooth." Strangely enough, the Israelites were allowed to keep slaves in this curious form of society, expressly allowed by the Lord. Nobody asked the slaves what they thought. The Promised Land, in which milk and honey were supposed to flow, and which had been promised to the Israelites, first had to be scouted out and then later conquered. Moses sent his scouts into the Promised Land and had them spy out this longed-for goal of their travels. The scouts, however, were afraid of the peoples who were already living in the Promised Land:

And there we saw the giants, the sons of Anak which come of the giants: and we were in our own sight as grasshoppers, and so we were in their sight. (Numbers 13:33)

Naturally, the people "murmured" again against Moses and his God—the murmuring had no end. Two hundred and fifty Levites ganged up and said, "Ye take too much upon you" (Numbers 16:3 ff). Of all people, it was the Levites who rebelled, the very team of people who had been allowed to transport the ark of the covenant and had maintained the "Ancient of Days." A great deal of resentment and anger seems to have built up. Moses ordered the three leaders of the group to come before him, and when they refused, he went to them—in order to kill them, together with their families, naturally with the help of the divine weapons technology:

And it came to pass, as he had made on end of speaking all these words, that the ground clove asunder that was under them:

And the earth opened her mouth, and swallowed them up, and their houses, and all the men that appertained unto Korah, and all their goods. They, and all that appertained to them, went down alive into the pit, and the earth closed upon them: and they perished from among the congregation. (Numbers 16:31 ff)

And what happened to the remainder of the 250 sons of Levi? "And there came a fire from the Lord, and consumed the two hundred and fifty men . . ." (Numbers 16:35).

So what are 250 dead compared to the innumerable tribes that the men of Moses destroyed—often with the help of extraordinary magic from their God? At least, this is what the Bible says. Whether things really happened that way is another matter. Moses's army then massacred all the males of the Midianites, and was also ordered to "kill every woman that hath known man by lying with him" (Numbers 31:17 ff). Naturally, each victory meant that enormous quantities of loot fell into the hands of the Israelites. The priests were supposed to deliver a certain part of this to the Lord as tribute. But even this was not enough, as the Lord also demanded people: "of which the Lord's tribute was thirty and two persons" (Numbers 32:40).

This story might sound rather terrible and incomprehensible, and of course, the theologians maintain that it was all meant symbolically. I have never found—anywhere—a single convincing argument for why the Lord would want loot or, even more crazily, what he needed people for. I am not just quoting a single passage from the Old Testament. Not at all. The Lord seems to be forever lusting after jewelry, precious stones, precious metals, delicately woven cloths, and yes, even seal skins.

Now, the texts of the Pentateuch (the first five books of the Old Testament) originate from different periods of time, and they definitely show up the signatures of various different authors. All the exegetes are agreed on this issue. In addition, things added later on were not originally part of the texts. Presumably, some of the merciless laws were invented later on and added to the five books by some fanatic. The trouble is that the scholars of the texts today can no longer determine which parts are the original texts. This makes me wonder even more about the fact that so many theologians require believers to look upon the texts in the Old Testament as "God's word." "Without exception, they are reports of the consummation of the Word of God. This pattern is generally applicable."[39]

We know from the traditional stories about Sodom and Gomorrah that the inhabitants of the two sinful cities placed no boundaries upon their sexual desires. Not only did they have intercourse with both sexes, but with animals too. Hence, the term *sodomy*. This perverse habit had to be radically eliminated. The corresponding punishments were appropriately severe:

Neither shalt thou lie with any beast to defile thyself therewith, it is confusion . . . And if a man lie with a beast, he shall surely be put to death: and ye shall slay the beast. And if a woman approacheth unto any beast, and lie down thereto, thou shalt kill the woman, and the beast: they shall surely be put to death; their blood shall be upon them. (Leviticus 18:23 ff and 20:15 ff)

Without a doubt, the Lord of the Israelites was familiar with modern hygiene, and he passed on his knowledge to his chosen people without any restrictions:

And when a man shall have in the skin of his flesh a rising, a scab, or bright spot, and it be in the skin of his flesh like the plague of leprosy, then he shall be brought unto Aaron the priest, or unto one of his sons the priests . . . And the priest shall look on the plague in the skin of the flesh: and when the hair in the plague is turned white, and the plague in sight be deeper than the skin of his flesh, it is a plague of leprosy . . . If the bright spot be white in the skin of the flesh, and in sight be not deeper than the skin, and the hair thereof be not turned white; then the priest shall shut him up him that hath the plague seven days . . .
(Leviticus 13:2 ff)

This instruction was about diagnosing diseases and, as in this case, keeping the patient in isolation. Modern-sounding instructions were given for total and careful disinfection. The rules of conduct left no margin for discretion:

[E]very bed, whereon he lieth that hath the issue, is unclean: and every thing, whereon he sitteth, shall be unclean, and whosoever toucheth his bed shall wash his clothes, and bathe himself in water . . . and he that toucheth the flesh of him that hath the issue shall wash his clothes, and bathe himself . . . and if the issue spit upon him that is clean: then he shall wash his clothes and bathe himself in water . . . and what saddle soever he rideth upon that hath the issue shall be unclean: and he that beareth any of those things shall wash his clothes . . . and the vessel of earth, that he toucheth, shall be broken . . .
(Leviticus 15:4 ff)

All these instructions regarding hygiene are dealt with in detail in Leviticus, chapters 13–16. They are perfect rules for combating disease. People with infectious diseases were not only excluded from the community, but tents and even entire houses became prohibited zones if a person with a particular set of symptoms of disease had been in it. The plaster was to be scraped off buildings, "the stones of it, and the timber thereof, and all the mortar of the house" and then carried away "out of the city into an unclean place" (Leviticus 14:45). The bodies of dead animals would not be touched, and even the High Priest Aaron should on no account go into the holy tent, unless he had thoroughly bathed himself beforehand. If Aaron did not adhere exactly to these rules for cleanliness and clothing given by the Lord, he would die, "that he die not" (Leviticus 16:2).

Harsh but true. Nothing "unclean" was to be allowed in the vicinity of the Lord, and certainly no smelly fellow. But the contradictions in the Old Testament scream out. On the one hand, Moses may never see the face of his Lord, so he never did come into direct contact with him; on the other hand, bathing and clothing rules were to be strictly enforced if anyone was to be near the Lord. In the Bible, all these hygiene rules apply only to the chosen people—only the Israelites are taught how to prevent the spread of infectious diseases, or even the outbreak of an epidemic. Other peoples did not seem to enjoy such privileges. It should be mentioned here, however, that the gods of other peoples, wherever the gods were living beings rather than statues, also demanded absolute physical cleanliness of their priests. One entered the holy of holies only after bathing and wearing pleasant-smelling, scrupulously clean clothes.

I will not discuss again, in this chapter, the fact that the Bible provides narratives of a technological nature that can be calculated and drawn according to the descriptions given, and point to anything but a metaphysical God (see my book, *Wir alle sind Kinder der Götter,* keyword Ezekiel).

So what remains of the God of the Old Testament after this listing of contradictions? An aged Jesuit with whom I once conversed suggested that God had perhaps given us a kind of thinking test. Will we find the answer? I think so, if one allows people to think freely and put two and two together. But every religious group tries to prevent exactly that. And I am not talking only about Christian groups! The concept of thinking for one's self is a horror in the minds of fanatical believers. Faith needs no proof. Faith lends security, even if reality is all chaos. Believing is not-wanting-to-know, as researching and thinking will inevitably lead to other answers. But thoughts cannot be killed off, just as the results of research cannot be. As long as humans exist, they will think. This flow is eternal, and even if groups who believe that only they are right succeed in stemming the flow, a fresh spring will always bubble up again, and a trickle will turn into a torrent.

In the Bible, God made eternal covenants with both Moses and Abraham. Historical research into the present times demonstrates that none of them was upheld. The return of God was prophesied several times, and a new kingdom was to begin. The only thing was, nothing happened. Religious zealots have prophesied a return of the Messiah in all manner of biblical passages. Not a single one of these quotes is correct. (Anyone who would like to read more about this should read chapter 3 of my book *The Return of the Gods.*) Exodus, chapter 34, demonstrates that God is a jealous god (verse 14) and that Moses should on no account make covenants with the inhabitants of another country. Where would the world be without international agreements? The Lord promised:

For I will cast out the nations before thee, and enlarge thy borders: neither shall any man desire thy land. (Exodus 34:24)

Where do "God's people" live today? Scattered across many continents, and the state of Israel is pressured by its neighbors. Orthodox Jews, who cling to every word of the Torah—if it serves them—expect the new kingdom to arrive sometime in the future. Tomorrow would be best. It does not seem to bother them that this kind of spiritual attitude makes a sensible agreement with their neighbors impossible.

I have already pointed out that Moses never saw his Lord face to face. But something seemed to have happened to Moses's face. When he came down from the holy mountain with the tablets of commandments, he "wist not that the skin of his face shone while he [the Lord] talked with him" (Exodus 34:29 ff). Was Moses suffering from the effects of radiation after his encounter with the Lord, which lasted some forty days? Peter Krassa suspected this more than fifty years ago.[40] If one follows the Old Testament, something strange really seemed to have happened to Moses:

And when Aaron and all the children of Israel saw Moses, behold, the skin of his face shone; and they were afraid to come nigh him . . . and till [when] Moses had done talking with them, he put a vail on his face. But when Moses went in before the Lord to speak with him, he took the vail off, until he came

out . . . and the children of Israel saw the face of Moses, that the
skin of Moses's face shone: and Moses put the vail upon his face
again, until he went in to speak with him. (Exodus 34:30 ff)

Veil on, veil off. The remainder of the text no longer mentions a veil. Did Moses's face look disfigured somehow after he had obtained his instructions from the Lord on the mountain? We know as little about this as we know about whether these biblical passages are genuine, or whether they have been invented and added by later writers, as many other things were. However, the narratives in the Bible are "without exception, reports of the consummation of the Word of God's. This pattern is universally applicable."[41]

If the Bible really consists entirely of "reports of the consummation of the Word of God's" and—according to theology professor Karl Rahner—the holy writ of the Old and New Testaments originated "from the same source" and this was planned "from times eternal" and for "final salvation," then believers would have to take the paragraphs in the Book of Revelation as true. The Book of Revelation has been added to the New Testament and is supposed to have been compiled by John the Evangelist. There, you can read about terrible plagues, which chastising angels will pour out over the Earth—naturally only on to unbelievers. The Lord is always demanding trials and punishments. But—what a surprise—after all the terrible times a new Heaven and a new Earth will arise:

And I saw a new heaven and a new earth: for the first heaven
and the first earth were passed away; and there was no more sea.
And I John saw the holy city, new Jerusalem, coming down from

God out of heaven . . . and the city was pure gold, like unto clear glass . . . and I saw no temple therein . . . and the city had no need of the sun, neither of the moon, to shine in it . . . (Revelation 21:1 ff)

I know people who believe in UFOs, who have been saying for years that extraterrestrials would turn up soon and lead a certain percentage of humans to another world. Scientists and politicians complain about this nonsense because it might lead to people giving up and blocking off the problems of our world. They are right, of course. They do not, however, appear to know where the source of this kind of thinking can be found: in the Book of Revelation in the Bible.

So where do we stand now? Where is this God who quite willingly allows himself to be fitted into all schools of thought? He seems not to be in the Bible or, for that matter, in any other holy or unholy text. Astrophysics has, during the last few decades, presented several models for the creation and nature of the Universe. All of these theories, developed by clever people with integrity, appear to contradict each other. According to Einstein's formulas, a resting universe cannot exist. This led physicist and astronomer George Gamow to the theory of the Big Bang in 1948. This idea was still thought of as incontestable when I went to school, because it could be proved by the red shift (Doppler effect) by Edwin Powell Hubble: the galaxies are rushing away from each other at increasing speed. This view stood until astronomers discovered galaxies that are so far away from us that they could no longer be covered by the umbrella of existing theories. Moreover, some of these galaxies should by now have reached a speed greater than that of light, which would contradict Einstein's theory. New theories had to be created. Physicist Andrei Linde of Stanford University developed the theory of a "bubble universe." According to this, just like in a bathtub full of mineral water, new bubbles keep on being created—new "Big Bangs." A universe of eternally exploding and newly creating bubbles. Naturally, this is not sufficient to grasp the universe, so new dimensions were necessary, and if there were none, they had to be created mathematically. If once twenty-five spatial dimensions were required in the complicated world of astrophysics, to help toss the salad, so at present, one manages with just ten. Even these ten are not accessible to the average citizen—they exist only in the heads and computers of scientists.

Astrophysicist Oskar Klein came up with the "string theory" (the universe is riddled with "strings of energy"). These strings may exist—nobody knows for sure—but they still did not explain the structure of the universe. So, physicist Edward Witten then created the theory of the vibrating membranes. Now the world had the "M-theory." *M* stands not only for "membrane" but also for "mysticism." Black holes were calculated mathematically, which contradicted older theories. Other astrophysicists not only puzzle about *how* the universe came into being, but whether it *ever* came into being. It had always been there. Incomprehensible! That is a word which does not exist in astrophysics, where the incomprehensible becomes possible. The main thing is that a new challenge to thinking is occupying the convolutions of the brain. And where did it come from, that thing that was always there? And how will it all end? Physicist Paul Davies has postulated a "Big Crunch" in addition to the "Big Bang." [42] Afterwards, the story of the universe begins anew.

Even the ancient Indians were familiar with that one, and it can be read in the Vedas.

What we are left with is a gigantic universe with trillions of stars and planets, which we now know is infinite—though we do not know whether it constantly renews itself and is born again somewhere, or whether it swallows up all its energy in the end. (This, of course, contradicts the law of the conservation of energy in physics.) Only one truth has emerged from all this. We humans on this tiny planet are like microbes compared with the universe, like microbes in a vast ocean.

Yet we still think we are so important that we seriously believe the grandiose Spirit of Creation only made up this game in order to visit our planet in a stinking, smoking, noisy, and dangerous vehicle. And then, to pick out among all humans a persistently complaining people as favorite—a favorite who for quite a long time, according to the descriptions of the Old Testament at any rate, would not believe in this God. And then he set about producing a nasty, tragic play, killing children and entire populations, and constantly—even with regard to events in the future—judging people and heaping punishments on them. And all of this in order to get stupid humankind to acknowledge him, to believe in him, and to love him. Not exactly what we know as Christian charity!

Where in this model is there any room left for a "good Lord," a loving God? The ancient, original Power, the ultimate First Spirit, which must have existed before the beginning of all Being, must have been a neuter, in human language terms: an "IT." IT existed before the Big Bang, before black holes and strings, before the bubble universe, and before all thoughts that we are capable of thinking. It is not possible for human understanding to grasp, to write about, or even to calculate this IT, except if, one day, this human understanding should be extended by some older intelligence. Still, I would at least like to try and imagine a model of this IT. In discussions, I have tried this with the following thought game:

Imagine a computer equipped with a hundred trillion "thought units"—"bits" in technical jargon. Then imagine the computer had developed personal consciousness. But this consciousness is firmly attached to the trillions of bits. If the computer then shot itself into the universe, this personal consciousness would be destroyed. Naturally, the brain of the computer knows this, because the computer knows everything. Knowing everything gets boring after a while, no matter whether there is such a thing as time or not. So, the computer decides to end this boredom and to store new experiences. What for? It already knows everything! The computer begins to number all its bits and to mark them in a particular sequence. And then it allows itself to explode. Big Bang. Trillions of bits, depending on their size, with varying speeds, shoot out into the vastness and emptiness of the universe. The original computer consciousness has been dissolved; it no longer exists. But the clever self-destructor has programmed the future after the explosion. All of the marked bits, with their individual bits of information, will eventually meet again in the center of the explosion. Every thought unit will take up its original place, and the personal consciousness of the super brain will be intact again—with an important difference. Every bit has experienced something from the time of the explosion until its return. Something happened. An additional experience, which did not exist before the break-up, is now part of that personal consciousness. The all-knowingness of the computer has been extended. Of course, this is a contradiction in terms, but—please bear with me—we are talking here about a thought model.

From the moment of the explosion until the moment of return, no bit knew that it was a tiny part of a greater consciousness. If a single bit had asked itself, during the long journey, "What is the meaning and the purpose of my super-fast journey?" or "Who created me?" or "Where do I come from?" there would have been no answer; that would be possible only if entire groups of thought units had found each other and perhaps had an inkling that something much greater must be behind it all. Nevertheless, every bit was the beginning and end of an act, a kind of creation, multiplied by the factor of new experience. I would have attained a great deal if this simplified thought model were a help in getting closer to the phenomenon of IT. We are all part of this Original Power IT. Only right at the end, Teilhard de Chardin's (1881–1955) "Omega Point,"[43] will we once more understand that we unite in ourselves the cause and result of Creation. I think it is fairly logical that IT, a synonym for the concept of God, must have existed before any kind of Big Bang. These thought models are not new; the only new feature is the up-to-date comparison with a computer. The fascinating thing is that ancient traditions know of similar ideas. John the Evangelist described Creation in the following way:

In the beginning was the Word, and the Word was with God, and the Word was God. All things were made by him; and without him was not anything made that was made. (John 1: 1–2)

We do not know from where John derived this brilliant insight. The sad thing is that the term *God* has been lumbered with impossible ideas for 2,000 years, ideas that are geared toward passing stories on to children and semi-savages. If the phenomenon of IT (God), however, has decided to transform into matter for a short while, then IT is itself Creation and simultaneously the product of its creation. Just like those computer bits, we too will find ourselves again in a unification. Together with trillions of other suns and the entirety of matter, we are microscopic particles of IT, which will all find their way back to the infinite cosmological community. All the philosophers torture themselves with the questions "Why?" "Where from?" "What for?" and yet "Knowledge," according to philosopher and theologian Professor Roland Puccetti, "need not necessarily be found by the scientific route. And it is a fact, that not a single so-called religious truth of note was ever derived in that way."[44]

A new millennium has begun. Where do we stand?

Humankind has been broken up into five great religions and thousands of rival sects.

Genetics, astronomy, and communications media have expanded our horizons to a degree never attained before. And there is no end in sight.

Sooner or later we will make contact with extraterrestrial intelligences. The speed of light will be overcome, contradicting all the theories.

How do we imagine the otherworldly? Do we want ourselves to be treated as intellectually inferior by an alien intelligence because we cannot use light switches on Saturdays (orthodox Jews)? Because we do not eat pork (Jews, Muslims)? Because we consider cows and fat rats to be holy (Hindus and related belief systems)? Or because we tortured our God and nailed him to a cross? I am in favor of announcing the end of the concept of many gods when we take that step into the third millennium. I would like to add that we are all tiny parts of the mighty IT for which religions have employed the term *God*. From this angle, every kind of racial discrimination would become complete humbug. We all belong to the same thing. And those religions with their self-righteousness, wars, and atrocities would have, in the end, led us to the path of enlightenment. The solution of that thinking challenge could consist of analyzing (I will be coming to this yet!) the contradictions in the Bible and other ancient texts. Finally, we would see the following task quite clearly: the Old Testament God was definitively not a metaphysical being as manifested in the Bible. The answer has to lie somewhere else, possibly out there in the universe. What should we do? Should we raze the temple, blow up the churches? No, of course not!

Where humans come together to praise Creation, there is a beneficial, strong sense of community. Just like being touched by the note from a tuning fork, we vibrate with a mutual presentiment of that magnificent being in space whom we call God. Temples and churches are places for contemplation, spaces for combined worship of the indefinable, of IT, for the grandiose Spirit of the Universe. These gathering places will remain necessary. All the rest is fairly superfluous.

CHAPTER 2

Lies Surrounding the Fátima Event

Moral indignation is the halo
of the hypocrite.

—HELMUT QUALTINGER

ON JUNE 26, 2000, the Vatican made public the "third secret of Fátima." Allegedly, it contained, in a symbolic language, information on persecution of the Church in the twentieth century and included a prediction of the assassination attempt on the pope. It is generally known that Pope John Paul II only narrowly escaped death on May 13, 1981, when assassin Ali Agca fired a pistol at the Holy Father in St. Peter's Square. The President of the Roman religious congregation, German Cardinal Joseph Ratzinger (later Pope

Benedict XVI), commented on the publication of the mystery with the following unctuous words:

> *The teaching of the Church distinguishes between "public revelation" and private revelations." There is not just a slight difference between them, but a considerable difference. The term "public revelation" refers to acts of revelation by God that are intended for the whole of humankind and the expression of which is to be found in the two-part Bible consisting of the Old and New Testaments. "Revelation" is the term used because God has revealed himself, step by step, to humans, up to the point where he became human himself, in order to draw the whole world to himself and become one with it, through his son Jesus Christ who became a man. And because God is One, the course of history in which he has joined humankind is a single one that is applicable to all times and attained fulfilment with the life, death and resurrection of Jesus Christ. The authority of "private revelations" is substantially different from that of a "public revelation."*[1]

He then goes on to inform us that a private revelation refers to the Faith and the "certainty" that God is speaking. The private revelation was intended as an aid to Faith. The measure and quality of a private revelation were a pointer to Christ himself.

> *If the "private revelation" should lead away from Christ . . . or should even set itself up as a different or better order, as more important than the gospel itself, then it is certain not to have originated from the Holy Ghost which, of course, leads us into the Gospel and not away from it.*[2]

What abstruse logic. If the omnipresent God makes a distinction between private and public, then a private revelation should also come from God. Not so, says the deeply pious cardinal. A private revelation can only come from God "if it leads into the Gospel." Do I infer from this that the opposition, the Devil, also gives private revelations?

Worldwide expectations about the contents of the third secret of Fátima were high, as in 1960 the pope had said he was unable to publish the secret because it concerned "our Faith." In 1980, Pope John Paul II declared to astonished journalists in Fulda

> *Due to the serious content, my predecessors in the Holy Office preferred a diplomatic version. Moreover, it should be sufficient for every Christian to know the following: if one were to read that oceans were to flood entire parts of the Earth, that humans would be gathered to their fathers from one minute to the next, in their millions, then one should really no longer yearn for a public declaration of this secret . . . Pray and ask no more. Leave everything else to the Holy Mother of God.[3]*

We certainly would have expected some earth-shaking announcement after such serious statements. And what is really in the (alleged) third secret? No sensations, no end of the world, no oceans slopping over with millions of dead, not even anything that concerned "our Faith." In addition to that, the published text does not even tally with reality. Here is the version released by the Vatican:

> *I write in obedience to You, my God, who instructed me, through his Excellency, the Most Reverend Bishop of Leiria, and through Your and my Most Holy Mother.*
>
> *After the two parts which I have already described, we saw to the left and slightly above Our Lady, an angel holding a*

flaming sword in its left hand; the sword was shooting out sparks and flames, as if they were about to set the world alight; but the flames were extinguished when they came into contact with the radiance that streamed from the right hand of Our Dear Lady: the angel, pointing to the earth with his right hand cried with a loud voice: Repentance, repentance, repentance! Then, in a mighty light that is God, we saw "something that looks like the image in a mirror of a person passing," a bishop dressed in white, "we felt he was the Holy Father." Various other bishops, priests, men and women of different orders climbed a steep hill, on the top of which stood a huge cross made of rough wood, like cork oak with the bark. Before arriving there, the Holy Father went through a large city that was half destroyed, and half trembling, with a wavering step, depressed with pain and anxiety, he prayed for the souls of the corpses he saw on his way. When he reached the top of the hill, he fell to his knees at the foot of the cross. There he was killed by a group of soldiers who shot at him with firearms and arrows. In the same manner, gradually, all the bishops, priests, people of orders and various secular people, men and women of different classes and positions died too. Beneath the two arms of the cross stood two angels, each one had a crystal watering can in its hand, in which they collected the blood of the martyrs and with this blood they watered the souls which approached God.

This public release by the Vatican—which is, after all, the highest instance of the Roman Catholic Church, to which an army of millions of believers belongs, and to whom this institution represents the highest instance of truth—can at best be half the truth, or half an untruth. Either the earlier popes lied when they made statements about the third secret of Fátima, or the reverend Cardinal

Ratzinger is lying now. In addition, the version released by the Vatican tells nothing about what happened in the past or in the present—not even the assassination attempt on the pope. Instead, it speaks of a "large city that was half destroyed," in which the Holy Father, together with many others, is shot dead. I am very sorry, Your Excellencies, but on May 13, 1981, when the pope was shot at, Rome was neither "half destroyed," nor did any shots hit any other people. And how does the President of the Roman congregation of believers interpret these contradictions?

According to Cardinal Ratzinger, this is about the keyword of the previous secrets, *salvare le anime* (saving the souls). This is expressed in the words *Penitenza, Penitenza, Penitenza* (Repentance, repentance, repentance). This reminds one of the beginning of the Gospel of Mark: "Repent and believe in the Gospel." The angel with the flaming sword represents the rules of the court. Human beings themselves had created and installed the flaming sword with their inventions. The whole show seen by the children of Fátima in a vision did not represent an "unalterable future," not a film showing the future as fixed, but a plan of how this (possible) future "could be turned into something positive." But how? Through repentance and understanding, of course. Cardinal Ratzinger: "This is why fatalistic interpretations of the secret completely miss the point, for example by saying that the assassin of the 13th of May, 1981, had been a tool employed by Fate for a divine plan, and he could, therefore, never have been able to act with free will . . ."

I should like to inquire humbly here, what had the assassin of May 13, 1981, to do with a "half destroyed" city? Or with a "group of soldiers"? And with the murder of many other people besides the pope?

The higher up the theologians are situated in the Church hierarchy, the more bewildering their way of thinking appears to be. Cardinal Ratzinger twists the vision of the future announced in the secret into a vague picture of the past. His commentary runs as follows:

> *The Pope is walking in front of the others, trembling and suffering because of the horrors surrounding him. Not only are the houses in this city partly in ruins, but his path leads past corpses of those killed. The path of the Church is described as a path to the cross . . . One should see the history of an entire century represented by this picture . . . In the vision, we should see the century ending now as a century of martyrs . . . a century of world wars and many localized wars . . . The figure of the Pope played a special role in all this. His weary climbing of the hill should stand for a group of several popes . . . In the vision, the Pope is also murdered on this road of martyrs. Should not the Pope, after looking at the text of the third secret after the assassination attempt of the 13th of May, 1981, have recognized his own fortune in this? He had been very close to death and had described his survival with the following words, ". . . it was a motherly hand that directed the flight-path of the bullet, and allowed the Pope who was fighting for his life, to stand still on the threshold of death" (statement by the Pope on the 13th of May, 1994). The fact that a "mano materna" (motherly hand) had, in the end, diverted the bullet, only shows once again that there is no unalterable fate, that faith and prayer are real powers that can interfere with history, and that, in the end, prayer is stronger than the patrons, faith is mightier than divisions.[4]*

What is presented here to the public really is a bit much. The "half destroyed" city is twisted and placed in the past century; the priests and members of orders *not* murdered at the time of the assassination attempt are transformed into martyrs of the past; the "flaming sword" is compared with human inventions; and finally, the bullet, which did *not* kill the pope, has been diverted by Mother Mary. Moreover, according to this commentary, the pope had read the third secret of Fátima after the assassination attempt of 1981, whereas he had, in reality, already made a public statement about it in 1980.

How does such an attitude of mind come about? The Mother of God in person is supposed to have appeared in visions to the children of Fátima. Which Mother of God? What really happened in Fátima in 1917? And how did these messages—or secrets—come together? What could the first and second secrets tell us, if the third one has been falsified?

Some might say that all of this originates in the imagination; it is an illusion. Others may argue that it represents a falsification of Church history for some 1,900 years. But let us proceed in the proper sequence.

I hope I made it clear in the first chapter that the Holy Writ of the Old Testament is a collection of contradictions unworthy of a metaphysical divine being, and which was created at different times and compiled by various authors. Christianity is based on the Old Testament and the New Testament. Remember, the texts of the Old and New Testaments are supposed to be derived from the same source. According to theology, God had made a special covenant with the people of Israel, which had been planned from time immemorial as the prologue to Christ's appearance.[5] Correspondingly, the New Testament is the continuation of the Old Testament. So who actually compiled the New Testament? Who wrote it? The good Lord?

Readers who are familiar with my work will, I hope, excuse me if I quote from one of my earlier books: We are dealing here with the beginnings of the unbelievable story about Fátima.[6]

Every believing Christian is convinced that the Bible is and contains the "Word of God." As for the gospels, there is a general belief that the followers of Jesus of Nazareth wrote down, so to speak, the speeches, rules for life, and prophecies he made. One is of the opinion that the evangelists had experienced the wanderings and miracles of their Master and had noted them down in a chronicle not long afterward. This "chronicle" was given a name: "the original texts."

In fact—and every theologian with a few years of higher education knows this—nothing about this is true. Those much-consulted original texts, so productive in theological sophistry, do not really exist. So what do we have? We have transcripts, copies that were all, without exception, created between the fourth and tenth centuries AD. And these copies, of which there are approximately 1,500, are in turn copies of copies, and not a single copy corresponds with another. More than 80,000 (eighty thousand!) variations have been counted. There is not a single page of these alleged "original texts" that does not come up with contradictions. The verses were drafted differently, from one copy to the next, according to the feelings of the copyists and appropriately adapted to the requirements of their times. These biblical "original texts" are teeming with thousands upon thousands of easily detectable mistakes. The most well-known "original text," the *Codex Sinaiticus* (which originated in the fourth century, just like the *Codex Vaticanus*), was discovered in a monastery in 1844. It contains no fewer than 16,000 (sixteen thousand!) corrections, which go back to at least seven authors of the corrections. Some passages were changed several times and replaced by a new passage of "original text." Dr. Friedrich Delitzsch, a first-class expert, has discovered 3,000 copy errors alone in the "original text."[7] This is all understandable if one considers that *none* of the evangelists was a contemporary of Jesus, and *no* contemporary ever compiled an eyewitness account. It was not until after the destruction of Jerusalem by Roman Emperor Titus (AD 39–81) in AD 70 that anyone began to compile texts about Jesus and his team. The evangelist Mark, of the first gospel of the New Testament, must have written his version at the very earliest forty years after his Master's death on the cross. Even the church fathers of the first centuries AD were at least agreed on the fact that the "original texts" were forgeries. They quite openly speak of "inserting, violating, destroying, improving, spoiling, extinguishing." But that is all a long time ago, and all the quibbling really does not alter the objective facts of the case. Specialist Dr. Robert Kehl, from Zurich, has commented:

It occurred often enough that the same passage was corrected or corrected back to the opposite meaning by one correcting copyist or the other, all depending on which dogmatic version was being represented by the school in question. These

*individual corrections, but even more the planned correc-
tions, have created a total textual chaos that can no longer
be disentangled.*[8]

These are the facts that one dare not admit to the believers.
What did Fátima have to do with all of this? The Mother of
God, Jesus's mother, is supposed to have appeared in Fátima.
It was *she* who appeared to the children of Fátima, *she* who gave
her message—the three secrets—to the children. How did
Christianity come to have a Mother of God? It all began with
the councils. In AD 325, Emperor Constantine (c. 274–337)
called the first council of the early Christian world in Nicaea.
The manner in which Constantine chose the 318 bishops who
were to attend had nothing to do with religion. It was pure
power politics. The emperor himself (who was not a baptized
Christian at the time; he received baptism on his deathbed!)
personally presided over the council. In true imperial style, he
let it be known that his will was Church law. The top shepherds
even accepted this unbaptized man as the "universal bishop,"
who naturally took part in all voting. Constantine actually had
not a clue about the teachings of Jesus. He was a follower of
the Sun cult of Mithras (an ancient Persian god of light). He
was depicted on coins and worshipped as the *sol invictus* (the
Unconquerable Sun) way into Christian times. When he gave
his name to the old Greek trading port Byzantium and made
Constantinople—present-day Istanbul—the capital of the
Roman Empire, with no trace of Christian humility, he had a
huge pillar erected to himself for the dedication. On top of the
pillar was a statue of the emperor as the Unconquerable Sun.
Constantine by no means abolished slavery, and even decreed
that slaves who were caught stealing food should have molten

lead poured into their mouths. He even allowed parents to sell their children in times of need.

And which decisions of Church policy did he become involved with? Up until the Council of Nicaea, the opinion of Arius of Alexandria was generally accepted: God and Christ were *not* identical in nature, but only similar. Constantine forced the council to decide in favor of the identical nature of God the Father and Jesus. This became Church dogma (doctrine of faith) by supreme imperial decree. This is how we got the idea that Jesus was identical with God. Based on this, the bishops then passed the Nicaean Creed through election by acclamation.

Constantine, the non-Christian, performed another enormous service to the Church. Up to that time, the burial site of Jesus was unknown. In 326, the emperor discovered the tomb of Jesus (who had just been acclaimed as God-like) by "divine inspiration."

Four years later, he had the Church of the Holy Sepulchre built in Jerusalem. This wondrous discovery did not, however, prevent the emperor from having some of his closest relatives murdered in the same year, among them his son Crispus, his wife Fausta—whom he had dipped in boiling water—and his father-in-law Maximilian, whom he forced to commit suicide. This is what the emperor and Pontifex was like, the one who managed the Nicaean Creed and then declared to the Christian communities in a circular that the votes of the 318 bishops were "God's judgment." Constantine, who was also given the epithet "the Great," was finally elevated to sainthood by the Armenian, Greek, and Russian Churches.

The second council took place in Constantinople in 381 and was called by Emperor Theodosius I (347–395). He too was decorated by the Church with the epithet "the Great." This Roman Imperator was not lacking in the same moral qualities as his colleague Constantine. He was, as history proves, a real old slave driver who imposed unbearable burdens on the poor. Those who would not comply were tortured. In 390, just ten years after the council, he had 7,000 rebellious citizens killed in a terrible bloodbath in the circus of the city of Thessalonike (Saloniki). This Emperor Theodosius declared the Christian teaching to be the state religion (hence "the Great"!). He ordered his Bishop Ambrosius of Milan to have all pagan shrines and temples destroyed, and whoever refused to be baptized was slaughtered.

And what happened at the second Council of Constantinople? The gathering decided on the teaching of the Trinity of the Father, the Son, and the Holy Spirit. This became the Nicaean-Constantinopolitan Creed. And here's a titbit for theological gourmets—the idea of the identical nature of God and Jesus, determined in Nicaea, now became the identical nature of the Father, Son, and Holy Ghost. The Church is still nurtured by the Trinity to this day.

The next council took place in Ephesus in 431 and was called jointly by the East Roman Emperor Theodosius II (401–450) and the West Roman Emperor Valentianus III (419–455). These two emperors did not bother themselves with worldly or spiritual problems, as they were both playboys. Consequently, they rarely graced the council with their presence.

Theodosius II was a weakling who was completely under the thumb of his older, power-crazy, scheming shrew of a sister, Pulcheria. She was, for a time, her brother's regent and boasted, on every suitable and unsuitable occasion, about her virginity (which her contemporaries merely smiled about). His colleague, the West Roman Emperor Valentianus, was under the guardianship of his mother, Galla Placidia, which ended in murder. Not exactly models of Christian behavior.

So, what did the Council of Ephesus decide? It decided on the Worship of Mary as the Mother of God. She was given the title *Bearer of God.* This was not due to inspiration from a spirit; it was a politically motivated act. The reason? Ephesus was the center of the worship of the Mother Goddess Artemis. The decision was intended to deflect existing mother goddesses from other religions and unite their worship in that of the Christian religion. Immediately after the declaration by the council, statues of Artemis were fitted with haloes and their names were changed to "Mother of God" and "Bearer of God." Most of the other religions, which were older than Christianity, were already familiar with "mother goddesses" who had, naturally, all not conceived in the normal way. Some god or the other was always involved. For this reason, a virginal birth was also inevitable for Mary. She was supposed to have conceived through an angel called Gabri-El; Gabri-El simply means "man of God."

And where did the name Mary come from? The older sister of Moses, the woman who had pointed out the floating basket containing the baby to Pharaoh's daughter, was called Mirjam (Mary). Even the Koran, the holy book of Muslims, which was written about six hundred years after the birth of Christ, reports the virginal birth by Mary:

Consider also in the Book [the Koran] the story of Mary. When she once retreated from her family to a place in the east, and covered herself with a veil, we sent our spirit [the angel Gabriel] in the form of a well-built man. She said, "I am afraid of you and seek refuge from you with the Merciful One. If you fear him too, do not approach me." He answered, "I have been sent by your Lord, to give you a holy son." But she answered, "How can I have a son when no man has known me, and I am not a whore?" He answered, "It will still be so; for your Lord has spoken, "This is easy for me. We will make him [the son] a won-drous sign for humankind, and he will be a proof of our mercy." So the matter is firmly decided." (190 Sura, 17 ff)[9]

A few verses on, we find, "she then came to her people with the child in her arms, and they said, "O Mary [Mirjam], you have done a strange thing! O sister of Aaron, your father was truly no bad man and your mother was no whore."

The virginal birth is confirmed in the 66th Sura, verse 12, "Mary [Mirjam] too, the daughter of Amran [was an example to them]. She preserved her chastity and we breathed our spirit into her . . ."

The Koran was announced in the Arabic language from around 610 to 632, the year that is often cited as that of the prophet Mohammed's death. According to Islamic history, the prophet Mohammed received revelations from Allah during the course of a total of twenty-three years. Allah is the Arabic name of the one God. In the Koran, as Mohammed emphasizes, Allah confirms his Word, which he sent earlier. This means that the third Sura emphatically recognizes the

Jewish Torah and the Christian gospels as prophets' words. The only major difference is now that the Koran represents the most up-to-date revelation of God and, therefore, the earlier prophets' words have been at least partly overtaken:

> *We believe in Allah and in what he sent us, and in what he revealed to Abraham, Ishmael, Isaac, Jacob and the tribes, and in what the Lord revealed to Moses, Jesus and the other prophets; we make no difference between any of these. We are Muslims [subjects of Allah]. Whosoever seeks a religion other than Islam—may he never adhere to it—for he shall surely be numbered among the lost in the future life. (3rd Sura, 84–85)*

According to the Mohammedan concept, Islam is the one and only right religion, because Mohammed was the last—or newest—prophet to receive God's word. Catholic theologians see this in exactly the opposite way. Because Islam considers it is the only true religion, the Koran demands of its believers, "Do not strike up friendship with those who are not of your religion" (3rd Sura, 117). In the Koran, Mary conceived as a virgin but never managed to get to Heaven. And Jesus is a prophet, but on no account God's son:

> *It is unseemly for Allah to have had a son. (19th Sura, 35)*

The name Mary (Mirjam, Maya) appears again at the birth of the Buddha. The Buddha was born of a virginal queen called Maya. The only thing is that this event took place centuries *before* the creation of Christianity.

Mary was not only elevated through the councils, but even more emphatically by the later popes. In 1854, Pope Pius IX announced that the Mother of Jesus had conceived Jesus "immaculately," and free of the Church's "original sin."

In 1950, Pius XII topped this. He elevated the Ascension of Mary to a dogma (a prerequisite article of faith). The Mother of Jesus, according to the dogma, had ascended into Heaven "body and soul." In a frontal opposition to Islam, on November 18, 1965, the Catholic Church announced, formally and highly officially, in the "dogmatic constitution":

That *God was the source* of the Bible,

That the Bible was holy, *in all its parts*,

That the Bible had been compiled *in all its parts* under the influence of the Holy Ghost,

That *everything* declared by the inspired compilers of the Bible had to be considered as written by the Holy Ghost, and

That the Bible teaches with *certainty*, *faithfully* and *without error.*

Three years later, in the solemn credo of Pope Paul VI on June 30, 1968, the following was explicitly emphasized:

the Catholic Church was the only true Church,

the Catholic Church alone proclaimed the infallible truth,

the Catholic Church was necessary for salvation,

the full treasury of heavenly riches had been entrusted to the Catholic Church,

the Catholic Church alone was the true inheritor of divine promise,

the Catholic Church alone was in possession of the Spirit of Christ,

the Catholic Church alone had been entrusted with the infallible chair of teaching,

the Catholic Church alone was in possession of the full and entire truth.

This solemn credo of Pope Paul VI was issued more than fifty years ago. Since then, the dignitaries of the Church have spoken innumerable times with the renegades from other churches, and the ecumenical movement was, and is, in. The followers everywhere are led to believe that the churches are stretching out their hands to each other and finally giving up on their unspeakable self-righteousness. Don't you believe it! In the autumn of 2000, the Catholic Church again declared itself to be unique and superior to all other churches. German newspaper *Die Welt* wrote:

> *The Catholic Church, in a recently published declaration, has described itself as the only true Church of Christ and thereby contradicted equality among different directions of faith. In the declaration Dominus Jesus (Jesus the Lord) compiled by the Catholic congregation of faith under the leadership of Cardinal Joseph Ratzinger, it is stressed that there is only one Church of Christ, the Catholic Church, and that it is led by the Pope, the successor of Holy St. Peter, and by the bishops.*[10]

Logically, the Council of Evangelical Churches of Germany (EKD) reacted badly to this stubborn one-sidedness by Rome. The chairman of the EKD described the declaration as a "setback for the ecumenical movement" and added that "the signals from Rome have stagnated." This did not in the least hinder the chairman of the German Bishops Conferences, the Catholic Karl Lehmann, from now quite openly and publicly insisting that there was only one true Church— namely, "the holy, Catholic and apostolic" one.

Non-Catholics or non-Christians may say to themselves, what on Earth has this to do with the third secret of Fátima?

What does it matter—what do we care about this theological self-righteousness within the Christian communities? Well, to be honest, it need not interest anybody, but it does affect the whole of humankind, because if one religion vaingloriously sets itself above all others, it does concern those other religions too. And this, in turn, concerns all human beings because the individual is part of his or her state system, and this is enmeshed with the ruling religion. Religions exercise power. And Fátima stands and falls with the Catholic religion and their Mother of God, because if the religion is false, then no Mother of God can appear and announce an earth-shaking secret. The imagined concepts that seem to exist in the brains of the current teachers in the Vatican can only either make one shudder or shake one's head and move on. Cardinal Ratzinger actually said that Christ was the Messiah of Israel and that the Jews should recognize Jesus (and therewith the Catholic religion as the only true one).[11]

Whom should the beleaguered believer now trust? Catholic Christians all over the world are duty-bound to believe in Mary as the "immaculate" conception, who ascended into Heaven and is the Mother of God. She is, so to speak, the heavenly deputy of her divine son, Jesus. And this most high female person in Heaven appeared to the children of Fátima in order to transmit secret messages to them. Upon my soul! But then, nothing is impossible in Heaven.

What really happened in Fátima? On the 13th of every month from May to October 1917, three shepherd children in Fátima (in the province of Estremadura, Portugal) experienced visions of Mary. The "Mother of God of the Rosary" appeared to them as a woman dressed in white with a wreath of stars around her head.[12] The children spoke of these visions vividly and with enthusiasm. During the summer and autumn of 1917, they were *the* most important events, even far beyond Portugal.

Now, visions of Mary had occurred before all over the world, but those of Fátima were different from all the others. The Mother of God commanded the children to come back to the same *place every month, on the same day, at the same time.* They did this, and more and more people accompanied the children out on to the field. The other people present did not experience any visions, but they were able to watch the three children suddenly sink to their knees, see their faces become transfigured, and observe how they evidently were talking with someone "up there."

We should, therefore, not be surprised to hear that a huge procession of about 70,000 people went on a pilgrimage out to the field on October 13, 1917, as the Mother of God had announced a miracle. That day, it rained in torrents—miserable conditions for something miraculous. But suddenly, the clouds opened up, a patch of blue sky appeared, and the "sun miracle of Fátima" began.[13, 14]

The Sun began to tremble and to sway. It made abrupt movements to the left and right, and finally began spinning about itself like a gigantic fiery wheel at great speed. Green, red, blue, and violet cascades of color shot out of the celestial body and bathed the landscape in an unreal, even an unearthly light, it was said. Seventy thousand people, among them journalists, witnessed this event and afterward confirmed that the Sun had stood still for some minutes, as if it had wanted to allow the people a pause for rest. Then the fantastic fireworks began again. It was indescribable, according to the witnesses. After a second pause for rest, the Sun dance began again for a third time with the same splendid appearance. In total, the miracle of the Sun lasted about twelve minutes and was observed within a circle of about 40 kilometers.

Today, the glassmakers in the Basilica at Fátima still depict this miracle of the Sun in glass. In spite of initial state measures to suppress the idea, Fátima became the goal for innumerable pilgrimages. To this day, it belongs among the most important places of pilgrimage in the world. On the first and last days of the visions, on May 13 and October 13 every year, Fátima resembles a gigantic garden of expectation. Thousands hope for a vision, for a miracle; what would please them most would be to see the miracle of the Sun again. This is true even of the popes, who have often traveled to Fátima. Never on any old day, but always on the 13th of a month.

Three children—Jacinta Martos and Francisco and Lucia Santos—had these visions "of the Dear Lady of Fátima" and simultaneously received her words, seemingly telepathically in their brains. The boy, Francisco, died on April 4, 1919, when he was nearly eleven years old. Miracles still happen in his name in Fátima. The girl Jacinta also died young. Only Lucia survived. She entered the monastery convent of Saint Theresa of Coimbra, where she died just short of her ninety-eighth birthday in 2005. If one can believe the versions of the Church, the nun Lucia did not write down the second secret of Fátima until June 13, 1929, and only revealed the third one on August 31, 1941—twenty-four years *after* the command of the Mother of God. Why so late?

The seer-children of Fatima.

The children are supposed to have seen Hell's fires in the first secret. "Our Lady showed us a giant sea of fire, which appeared to be deep in the Earth. We saw the Devil and the souls immersed in this fire, as if they were transparent, black or brown glowing coals in the shape of humans . . ."

This declaration by the seer-children is diametrically opposed to a declaration by Pope John Paul II. In July 1999, he clearly explained what we should expect of Paradise and of Hell. This was published in the mouthpiece of the Jesuit Order, *Civilta Cattolica*. Paradise, declared the Holy Father, was not a place above the clouds where angels play harps, but a state of being that occurs after death. In St. Peter's Square, the aged pontifex explained to pilgrims that Paradise was a living, personal relationship with the Holy Trinity. It was a "blessed community of those who had remained loyal to Jesus Christ during their lifetime." After clearing this one up, the pope logically had to state a position with respect to Hell. It was not "a realm in which the souls of the damned fry in eternal fires and are tortured in other ways." No, according to John Paul II, Hell is a "state of being, in which those end up who have constantly rejected God and have consciously done evil."[15] These individuals were doomed never to attain the joy of being in the presence of God.

How could the children of Fátima have looked into Hell, which, according to the papal declaration, does not exist?

In the second secret, the lady with the crown of stars announced that a great kingdom would be destroyed if one did not finally acknowledge it worldwide and worship it, and if human beings did not finally give up their erroneous teachings. The popes—or some cardinals, nothing seems certain about this—turned this "great kingdom" into Russia, even though the original text of the seer Lucia never mentions the word *Russia* anywhere. Pope Pius XII spoke of a kingdom in which, in ancient times, the "revered icon" was worshipped. We know that icons are not only revered in Russia but were worshipped during the first few centuries of the Christian Church. These interpretations seem embarrassingly reminiscent of the oracle of Delphi in ancient Greece. There, the filthy rich ruler Croesus asked the oracle whether or not he should engage in battle with the Persians. The Pythia of Delphi answered that if he crossed the river Halys, he would destroy a great kingdom. In 546 BC King Croesus blithely crossed the Halys with his troops, expecting victory, and was thoroughly beaten by the Persians. The "great kingdom" he destroyed was his own.

In the second secret of Fátima, there was a further announcement that under the pontificate of Pope Pius XII a new, terrible world war would begin: "If you see a night illuminated by an unknown light, then you will know that this is the great sign given you by God, that he will punish the world for its misdeeds by war, starvation, persecutions of the Church and of the Holy Father."

In my lifetime, I cannot remember that any night was "illuminated by an unknown light," nor do I remember that the dreadful Second World War represented some kind of judgment or punishment that destroyed the godless. Russia (then the Soviet Union) belonged among the victorious powers, and Germany was ruined. Innumerable Catholic churches were destroyed too.

Now the third secret of Fátima is at hand and the dance of the veils begins once more. The nun Lucia is supposed to have written down the secret on August 31, 1941, and added to it on December 8, 1941. But then Lucia is not supposed to have written down her notes in neat copy until January 3, 1944, at "the instructions of His Excellency, the most reverend Bishop of Leiria, and the Holy Mother." The bishop sealed the envelope containing the secret and kept it in his safe for thirteen years. Not until April 4, 1957, did he hand over the sealed envelope to the secret archive of the Holy Office in Rome. The gracious bishop generously informed Sister Lucia of this fact.

It is unbelievable! Here we have a child who receives a mysterious but very important message from the Mother of God, the Queen of Heaven and highest representative of the Roman Church, in 1917. The child, who has meanwhile become a nun in a convent, does not write down any notes until twenty-four years later, and three years after that, these notes, "on the instructions of the bishop . . . and the Most Holy Mother," are written down neatly on paper. In spite of the explosive nature of the contents of this piece of writing, the bishop retains the papers for fully thirteen years in his possession before finally transferring them to the Holy Office in Rome. And what do the gentlemen of that secret circle do with it?

On August 1, 1959—a year and a half later!—the secret is passed on to the top man in the Church, Pope John XXIII, and this is all with the agreement of the "Most Reverend Cardinal Alfredo Ottavani and the Commissioner for the Holy Office, Father Pierre Paul Philippe O.P." Who is really the boss in the Vatican? The pope or some priests in the Holy Office? And why is "agreement" required to hand over such an important document to the top man in the Church? And why in 1959?

Because, we are told, the "Dear Lady of Fátima" had demanded that the secret be revealed to all humankind on October 17, 1960, forty-three years after the apparition at Fátima.

This is what Sister Lucia herself had written on the outside of the sealed envelope with the third secret. There, she had written that either the Patriarch of Lisbon or the Bishop of Leiria should open the envelope. Later, Sister Lucia said that it was not the lady who set the date in 1960, but she herself, "because I felt that one would not understand the message before 1960."

If this is true, a simple nun in a convent would have been the one who made the decision when a terribly important message, conveyed personally by the Queen of Heaven, was to be passed on to her earthly representatives. And what then do these earthly representatives do with this unique message? Pope John XXIII told the gentlemen of the Holy Office, "Let's wait. I will pray. I will let you know what I decide."[16]

And then Pope John XXIII decided to seal the envelope again, to give it back to the Holy Office, and *not* to reveal the secret to the world. The head priest of the Roman Church thinks he is cleverer and wiser than his own Mother of God, who must have known why she chose the seer-children to participate in her vision.

The next Pope, Paul VI, read the secret together with the Substitute, his Excellency Monsignore Angelo Dell'Acqua, on March 27, 1965—and decided again to give the envelope back to the Holy Office, with the advice *not* to publish the text. This is quite extraordinary! If the secret had been as simple as is now maintained, and in the form that it was finally published, there would not have been the slightest reason for Popes John XXIII and Paul VI *not* to release the text. The version I gave at the beginning of this chapter allegedly speaks of the martyrdom of the Church and the pope in the century *just passed*. This is according to the explanation given by Cardinal Ratzinger. What would have hindered the popes from making public a story that referred to the past?

It is not known when John Paul II first read the third secret of Fátima. It must have been *before* 1980; otherwise, he could not have spoken about it during his visit to Fulda in the same year. John Paul II asked to see the sealed envelope a second (or third?) time after the assassination attempt of May 13, 1981. On July 18, 1981, His Eminence, the Cardinal

Prefect of the Congregation, Franjo Seper, handed over two envelopes to His Excellency Monsignore Eduardo Martinez Somalo: one white envelope that contained the original Portuguese text by Sister Lucia and an orange-colored one, in which was the Italian translation. The pope opened the explosive envelopes and then gave them back to the Holy Office (via Martinez).[17]

Once more, there was no publication to the world. The assassination attempt on the pope had taken place two months before; the Holy Father had survived and was recuperating in his chambers in the Vatican. What conclusive reasons could he have given now not to reveal the secret? If one believes the revelation, everything had already happened that was foreseen in the secret. But it was not until the year 2000 that the pope decided the secret ought to be revealed to the world. Why, if the contents were so harmless, was it necessary finally to publish the secret?

Because the whole story does not stick. As early as 1983, German news magazine *Der Spiegel* wrote:

> *There is proof in books that have yellowed with age that it was not humankind but the Vatican who had to be afraid of the publication of the secret.*[18]

The popes decidedly helped to make a phenomenal place of pilgrimage out of the former little village of Fátima. In the middle of the Second World War, on October 17, 1942, Pope Pius XII had dedicated Fátima to the Immaculate Heart of Mary. On May 13, 1982, Pope John Paul II visited Fátima and celebrated mass in front of 100,000 believers, during which the Holy Mother of God, the Immaculate Conception, was worshipped with great fervor. On April 19, 2000, Pope John Paul II wrote the following letter to the aged nun Lucia in the Convent of Coimbra:

> *On the joyous occasion of these days of the celebration of Easter, I greet you with the blessing that the Resurrected One bestowed upon his disciples, "Peace be with you!" I am looking forward to meeting you on the yearned for day of the beatification of Francisco and Jacinta, which, God willing, will take place on next 13th of May. As there will be no time on that day for a conversation, but only for a brief greeting, I have instructed His Excellency Monsignore Tarcisio Bertone, the Secretary for the Congregation for the Teaching of the Faith, to visit you and speak to you. This Congregation works together closely with the Pope to protect the true Catholic Faith, and as you will know, has since 1957, preserved your hand-written letter which contains the third part of the secret revealed on the 13th of July, 1917, in the Cova da Iria, Fátima. Monsignore Bertone, who will be accompanied by His Excellency Monsignore Serafim de Sousa Ferreira e Silva, the Bishop of Leiria, will come to you in my name, to ask you some questions regarding the interpretation of the "third secret." Reverend Sister Maria Lucia, please speak openly and honestly with Monsignore Bertone who will personally inform me of your answers.*

> *I pray most profoundly to the Mother of the Resurrected One for you, for the Community of Coimbra and for the entire Church. May Mary, the Mother of Humankind on the pilgrim's path, always hold us close to Jesus, her beloved son, our brother, the Lord of Life and Splendor.*

> *With a special apostolic blessing,*

> *John Paul II*[19]

More than one hundred years have passed since the secrets were revealed to the children of Fátima. Pope John Paul II knew the third secret for at least eighteen years, yet not until the year 2000 did the Holy Father send a high-ranking emissary to the convent of Coimbra to pose "a few questions regarding the interpretation of the third secret" to the old and venerable nun Lucia.

Of course, nobody knows what was really discussed during that conversation. The Vatican merely stated that Sister Lucia had identified the paper on which the secret had been scribbled down as her own. And she had said, that "the lady" (the Mother of God) had not given the name of the pope in question in the vision. "We did not know whether it was Benedict XV, or Pius II, or Paul VI, or John Paul II, but it was the Pope who was suffering and also caused us to suffer."[20]

Whoever believes this is insinuating that the good Lord, or the Mother of God, is incapable of manifesting clearly. This would mean it was not possible for the Divine Power to transmit clearly pictures and messages into the brains of children. Some questions need to be asked to disperse the fog around the happenings of Fátima:

Did anything really happen in Fátima, or was the whole thing an invention of the seer-children?

Why should the divine Almighty transmit messages to the brains of children and not to adults or, in our times, directly via electronic media?

Who or what was manifested?

Is the Vatican lying?

If so, why?

The only survivor of the events of the year 1917 was the nun Lucia. One may disagree about her credibility, as it is a fact that she only wrote down her grandiose experience twenty-four years after the event. There is, however, no disagreement about the Sun miracle of Fátima, for it was, after all, witnessed by 70,000 people. What happened to this mass of people on October 13, 1917, became part of the press reports. It was photographed, albeit only in black and white. There is no way one can get past the Sun miracle; something definitely out of the ordinary took place in Fátima. Those 70,000 witnesses were not all suffering from sensory disorders. Skeptical scientists and critical journalists were able to witness it and, after all, it lasted a full twelve minutes. Moreover, this Sun miracle had been announced beforehand to the children of Fátima. To the exact day and minute. It was only *because* of this announcement that 70,000 people had set out to make the pilgrimage to the field. Ergo, Lucia *must* have received a message. But what did happen? And why did it happen through the children? I will have to explain a few things first, before penetrating to the heart of the matter.

Thousands observe the "Sun miracle" of Fatima.

Regretfully, I have never witnessed an apparition. Since the first time I stayed in Lourdes in 1964, however, I have understood that the phenomenon of apparitions really exists. I witnessed people in a state of ecstasy, heard them singing with suffering souls, and watched their great pain. More than 160 years ago, long before Fátima, a fourteen-year-old girl in Lourdes (France) witnessed the apparition of a white lady in a small rocky grotto. Since then, five million people yearly make the pilgrimage to Lourdes and pray fervently to the Mother of God. Scientifically verifiable miracle healings have resulted. How is this possible if the Mother of God is a mere invention of the Church, first decided upon and then announced at the Council of Ephesus?

The beginning is always a vision, an apparition, a meeting of individual or small groups of people with members of families of God(s). In the Christian occident, these events chiefly involve Mary, the Mother of Jesus. The apparitions are not of neutral spirits: no advice is given about what people should or should not do, or what is forbidden. Every personified apparition affirms himself or herself to be an emissary from Heaven and a divine messenger who has the power to help or destroy humankind. These apparitions interfere in religious and political matters, and they even get into the brains of entire warring groups. I will first sketch a few of these seers, places, and circumstances in order to explain the phenomenon.

In the spring of 1947, there was an apparition in Montichiari, 10 kilometers south of Brescia, in Italy. There, in the hospital chapel, a young nurse named Pierina Gilli saw a beautiful lady in a violet dress floating above the altar. The strange lady was crying. From her breast, without a drop of blood flowing from it, protruded three swords. The unknown lady said sadly, "Prayer—Sacrifice—Repentance."

Understandably, the pious Miss Pierina was confused. Were her eyes and mind deceiving her? Or was plain little Pierina dealing with a first vision? The miracle was repeated on July 13, 1947. This time, the beautiful unknown lady was dressed in white and the terrible swords were missing, but she was adorned with three roses—a white one, a red one, and a yellow one—all of which protruded from her breast. Shy and courageous at once, Pierina asked, "Who are you?" The lady smiled and answered gently, "I am the Mother of Jesus and the Mother of All . . . I want the 13th of July to be celebrated yearly in honor of the mystery of the rose [Rosa mystica]."[21] Slowly the apparition faded again.

This incomprehensible spectacle was repeated on October 22, and on November 16 and November 22, whereupon the strange lady solemnly promised to appear again at noon on December 8—not in the hospital chapel this time, but in the village church. The news about Pierina's strange experiences had traveled far beyond Montichiari and into the Lombardy countryside. No wonder, then, that on the December 8 several thousand people traveled to the village. The main person in this dramatic event, Pierina Gilli, had to be passed through the wall of people and into the church with a great deal of effort and gentle force. There, she prayed a rosary together with other believers and many curious people. Suddenly, she cried out: "Oh! The Madonna!"

Everyone became silent. But nobody saw a thing. That is, some were not quite certain that they hadn't seen something. At any rate, everyone's eyes were glued to Pierina, so as not to miss a word of her conversation with the Mother of God. The message was passed in brief whispered words out to the masses waiting outside the church.

They gathered that Pierina could see the Mother of God on a tall, white stair, and once again adorned with white, yellow, and red roses. With an otherworldly smile, the lady disclosed, "I am the immaculate Conception, I am Mary of the Mercies, Mother of my divine son Jesus Christ."

While descending the white stair, as in a stage show, she said to Pierina, "With this my coming to Montichiari, I wish henceforth to be called 'the Mystic Rose.'" When she got to the bottom steps, she prophesied, "Whoever prays on these bricks and sheds tears of repentance will find a sure ladder to Heaven, and will receive protection and mercy from my motherly heart."

For nineteen years nothing further happened. As is usual, Pierina was derided by some of the people and venerated as a saint by others. From December 8, 1947, onward, the church of Montichiari was the goal of believers in miracles and those seeking healing, because miracles upon miracles happened there, there was no doubt about it.

Pierina spent White Sunday, April 17, 1966, in the neighboring village of Fontanelle, only 3 kilometers away. While Pierina was resting on the steps of a small spring, suddenly and totally unexpectedly, the "Mystic Rose" floated above the water. It instructed Pierina to kiss the steps from top to bottom, three times, then order a crucifix to be erected on the left beside the bottom step. All the sick, so the apparition said, before taking water from the spring, should ask Jesus for forgiveness of their sins and kiss the crucifix. Pierina followed these instructions. On May 13, 1966, at 11:40, when about twenty people with Pierina were praying next to the spring, the "Mystic Rose" appeared once more and conveyed the following wish: "I wish that a comfortable basin be created here, so the sick can immerse themselves in the water." As she was now quite used to the apparition, Pierina asked the rose-adorned lady, "How should the spring be called?" The lady answered, "The Spring of Mercy." Pierina questioned her again: "What do you want to happen here in Fontanelle?" "Charitable works for the sick who will come here"[22] was the answer. Then, the "Mystic Rose" disappeared.

It is June 8, 1966; afternoon. More than 100 people are kneeling and praying beside the spring. Shortly after 15:00 hours, Pierina joins them. She asks the visitors to pray a rosary with her. Moments later, she interrupts her prayer and calls out, "Look up to the sky!" This time, some of the believers see a white lady floating about 6 meters above the spring.

The lady is carrying her three roses once again and asks that wafers for hosts be made out of the corn in the neighboring field. These hosts are to be taken to Fátima on October 13. Just as the mysterious lady is about to leave, Pierina asks her to stay. The lady actually turns and listens to Pierina telling her about the troubles of those present.

It is August 6, 1966; afternoon. More than 200 people are praying by the spring. At 14:30 hours, Pierina appears and again asks those present to pray a rosary with her. During this fourth rosary-mystery, Pierina interrupts, calling out, "Our Dear Lady is present!"

Conversations and prayers fall silent. Everyone is listening to Pierina conversing with a being that is invisible to them. When asked for further directions as to what should be done with the homemade hosts, the "Mystic Rose" asks that some of the grain should be sent to her "dearly beloved son Pope Paul," with the note that it had been blessed by her presence. Also, the remaining grain should be used to bake rolls and to distribute them in Fontanelle in memory of her coming.

Since then, one prays and hopes in Fontanelle as well as in Montichiari. All day and all night. Just as in many places where apparitions or visions have occurred. All in all, this is a classic example of this kind of apparition. A person, unknown until that moment, sees something, tells others, and the round of prayers begins. But how can a Mother of God manifest if, from a historical perspective, she never existed? How can the apparition state of itself that it is "the immaculate Conception" and "Mother of the divine son Jesus Christ" if both statements are false? Why does the strange lady appear first with swords in her breast, then with roses that appear to grow out of her body? Why should the Mother of God attach such importance to being called the "Mystic Rose"? And why does the "Rosa mystica" always stage its appearance wherever Pierina happens to be present? First in the hospital chapel, then in the village church, then in Fontanelle? Why should she not manifest again for nineteen years, and what benefit does the divine power derive from having the young Pierina kiss the steps three times? And finally, why has nothing at all happened for nearly sixty years? Is there some power out there playing about with us humans?

The method of circling around a problem for possibilities for solutions is not my invention. The explanation of curious phenomena requires methodical procedures, and the circumstances of the facts need to be determined.

I have spent more than fifty-five years dealing with apparitions of all kinds. When I began creating a case archive, I had no idea what an overwhelming mass of printed matter I would have to cope with. I had to be selective, which means I chose cases that would stand for many similar other ones, so that I would be able to offer a possible answer out of the sum of the characteristics. The fact that more than 40,000 (!) apparitions have been counted in the Christian world alone will give some idea of the polysemantic nature of the matter. One thing I very quickly noticed when looking at this material was that apparitions are not a problem of the present. They can be found throughout the history of humankind. One of the psychological explanations thus has the rug pulled out from under it by this observation. I repeatedly hear that apparitions occur in the brains of children, only because they cannot cope with the problems of our present times. A load of nonsense, is all I can say, based on my own experience.

On August 16 every year, a blood-soaked cloth is prayed to by believers in Iborra, Spain. This ritual has been going on since 1010. At that time, the most reverend gentleman Bernard Olivier, while ringing the bell during the consecration, had sudden doubts about whether the red wine really was transformed into Christ's blood. Suddenly, the red wine (or the blood) had increased in a mysterious way and had flowed down from the altar table onto the steps and onto the floor of the chapel. Horror gripped the churchgoers. A few resolute women fetched cloths and began to mop up the blood. Pope Sergius IV (1009–1012) permitted the public adoration of the bloody cloth of Iborra. And it has gone on to this day. It means that not only holy figures cause manifestations.

The pious Monsieur Thierry, the rector of Paris University, was murdered in Pirlemont, Brabant, in 1073. The brutal murderers threw his body into a murky pool of water. When search parties were combing the area looking for Monsieur Thierry, a wondrous light shone out of the pool. In thanks for this strange apparition, an artist painted on a wooden panel a picture of the Mother of God floating above water. In 1297, the picture was transferred to a new chapel. During the celebrations for the official consecration, the picture suddenly began to shine and was enveloped in light as of flames.[23] Hundreds witnessed it and some described it. No holy figure appeared during this phenomenon.

On a hill called Codol, 5 kilometers from Javita, near Valencia in Spain, a small throng of Christian warriors was fighting against an Islamic army, far superior in numbers, on February 23, 1239. Before the battle, six of the Christian chiefs asked for holy communion. They were just able to make confession, but were not able to receive the sacrament, because at that precise moment, the battle cry of the enemy resounded from the nearby castle of Chio and penetrated the church. The chiefs rushed to arm themselves. Full of fear that the Muslims could destroy the church, the priest hid away the altar cloth and hosts under a heap of stones. The Christian warriors carried the day. When the priest went to retrieve the altar cloth from its hiding place, six *bloody* hosts were stuck to it. But this was not all! The next day, the Muslims advanced with reinforcements. The situation seemed hopeless; the Christians had to retreat to the castle Chio, which they had taken the day before. Following a sudden hunch, the priest bound the cloth with the six bloody prints to a pole and waved it at the enemy from the top of the castle battlements. According to the legend, rays of light went out from the altar cloth that had such power, the greatly superior forces of the enemy fled.

Is this proof that apparitions are able to vanquish entire armies? Or is it only a pious legend? Since the thirteenth century, every traveler to Spain can visit the church of Daroca and check the altar cloth with the six bloody spots.[24] I should point out here, however, that the *opposite* has also occurred, according to legends, namely, that Christians armies took flight due to Muslim apparitions. Do divine powers sometimes help one side and sometimes the other? And do these wondrous events occur only in the Christian and Muslim worlds?

According to the legends, Rome was founded by Romulus and Remus, the twin sons of Mars. Romulus, who ruled in Rome from 753 to 716 BC, was once visited by the apparition of Servius Tullius (the sixth Roman king, 578–535 BC), son of Vulcan, who manifested in a "fiery glow above his head."[25] The god of healing, Asclepius, appeared in the temple of Epidauros (Greece) about as often as the chief consultant at the bedsides of our clinics. Naturally, countless miracles occurred in Epidauros, long before Christianity. The Roman lawgiver Numa Pompilius, Minos (King of Knossos), and Lycurgus (lawgiver of Sparta) generally received their creative ideas directly through apparitions of the gods. Aeneas, hero of the Trojan cycle of legends, appeared to his son Ascanius after his death, wearing full armor and with all his followers. The ancient Iranian founder of a religion, Zoroaster, who was active as a prophet c. 600 BC, received the decisive passages of his religious writings (Avesta) through several visions. Mohammed, the founder of Islam, who proclaimed Allah, received many of the revelations that were laid down in the Koran through visions.

And so it goes on. Visions or apparitions of all kinds influenced thinking throughout the history of humankind, right through to Fátima. What is particularly noticeable is that in 90 percent of the cases, it is children who are the recipients or transmitters of these transcendental phenomena. Actually, I find that rather logical. Children before puberty do not have many worries. Their opinions are not yet fixed, and their consciousness has not yet passed through the brainwashing process of the everyday grind. They still have their naïve inquisitiveness and child-like imagination.

I can well imagine that pictures can be projected into the minds of children and also that the information that goes with it can be transferred by telepathy. This would mean that apparitions were not objective, neither able to be photographed nor measurable, but still, from the child's point of view, they would be subjective and therefore clearly perceivable via the limbic system. The child will swear blind that he or she has perceived an apparition, while all others present have seen nothing. But how can the absurd thought be created in a brain, for example, that a mysterious lady wants to be called "Mystic Rose"? Are humans with such imaginings simply psychically disposed, or is the apparition with all accompanying manifestations simply something that has risen from the imagination? If it is pure fantasy, where do the accompanying manifestations come from, like the medical cures, or the Sun miracle of Fátima, which was witnessed by some 70,000 people? And if it is a "picture projected directly into the brain by telepathy," who is doing the projecting? Who is the sender of the thought transfer?

All apparitions are full of contradictions. In the case of apparitions of Mary, the Mother of God, she always refers to the power lent her by her son. If she does indeed have this power at her disposal and has the burning desire to be worshipped by believers all over the world, then why does she appear in such out-of-the-way places, and usually to poor little souls who are actually able to do very little to fulfill her desires? Places of pilgrimage like Fátima, Lourdes, or Guadalupe (in Mexico) are exceptions insofar as they are world-renowned centers for the worship of Mary. Most other apparitions have occurred with a minimum of publicity. Apparitions of Mary are also mainly a Catholic phenomenon. Believers of all other religions know very little about Mary as the Mother of God, or do not acknowledge her Ascension (into Heaven) in the flesh.

Every year, year after year, the pope gives his blessing *urbi et orbi* (to the city of Rome and to the world) on high church feast days from the balcony of his palace in Rome. Television stations transmit this highest papal blessing to the whole world, and a sea of 200,000 believers cheers in St. Peter's Square. If some divine power really wished to receive more worship than hitherto and desire that humans should do penance in some area of life, why then—please!—do they not launch a proper apparition right there in St, Peter's Square?

Things get even more bewildering. In September 2000, the *Welt am Sonntag* reported apparitions of Mary in Egypt.[26] The Holy Virgin had appeared several times above St. Mark's Church in the town of Assiut. At first, white doves had appeared, then a beam of light, which was allegedly so supernaturally bright and strong that observers had to look away. The official weekly of the orthodox Coptic Church in Egypt, *Watani*, reported that entire flocks of white pigeons had suddenly remained in the air above the dome of the church. These pigeons had unusually long feathers. After the pigeons came the brilliant beam of light and then the "Holy Virgin." Since then, there has been no end to the streams of pilgrims to Assiut. The believers march to the church of St. Mark to plead for the blessing of the Mother of God. According to several traditions, appearances of Mary occur again and again in Egypt. In this century alone, three of these apparitions were officially confirmed by the Coptic Church.

And under which umbrella do all *these* apparitions of Mary fit? The Mother of God, "ascended into Heaven" is, after all, one of the dogmas of the Roman Catholic Church. So, why does the highest female representative of the Catholic Church not stick to her very own church? Do Catholics not have an exclusive right to the Mother of God? Does she show herself to believers of other faiths? And why? No telepathic messages were transmitted at Assiut.

The first apparition of the Mother of God in the Americas occurred on December 9, 1531. The Spaniards had conquered Central America. A religious war was raging in Mexico, which was won by the Spanish. Hundreds of thousands of Mayans and Aztecs had been slaughtered; any kind of reconciliation between the two cultures seemed impossible. Then, early one morning in December 1531, Juan Diego, a fifty-one-year-old Indio, heard strange music that seemed to be coming from nowhere. Juan stared up and heard a voice from the sky that told him to climb up the hill called Tepeyac.

When he arrived at the top, he saw a beautiful lady whose robe shone like the Sun. The stones round about, even the rock on which the lady stood, sparkled and winked like gold and emeralds. "Listen to me, Juanito, the smallest of my sons, where do you want to go?" the voice asked him. Juan really wanted to get to the other side of the hill, but the lady bade him go to the Bishop of Mexico and to tell him about this encounter. The bishop would not believe a word of what the Indio told him. Juan went back to the hill and asked the lady, who had promptly appeared again, to give him something as evidence. The lady ordered Juan to pick flowers, wrap them in a cloak, and take them to the bishop.

Juan obeyed. Although the guards at the palace tried to dissuade him, Juan finally managed to penetrate to the bishop. There were other people in the room. Juan reported what he had been told by the lady and opened his cloak with the flowers. At that moment, a brilliant, blinding light appeared and Juan's cloak was transformed into a picture of the lady in front of all those present. She was wearing a shining blue cloak decorated with golden stars, and red and white rays shot out of the cloak.

Today, on the hill of Tepeyac stands the largest shrine to Mary in the whole of the Americas, the Nacional Basilica de la Santissima Maria del Guadalupe. Millions of believers pray to the Mother of God and stare at the colored cloth from 1531 that should not really exist. The cloth consists of agave fibers that decay rapidly and in the best cases last for about twenty years. But this cloth has been hanging above the main altar of the basilica for almost five hundred years. And that is not all. The cloth, which has been examined by experts, including painters at several universities, is in reality colorless. It contains no traces of color. Nevertheless, twenty million people every year see this colorful cloth. The constellations of stars on the blue mantle correspond to the forty-six stars that would have been visible above Mexico in the winter of 1531. And as microscopic photographs confirm, the eyes of the lady mirror images of the bishop and all those present in the room when Juan Diego opened his cloak full of flowers.

The colored cloth of Guadalupe, which in reality contains no colors.

I have been in the Basilica of Guadalupe, glided along the travelator with many other believers, and stared up in awe, like all the others, at the colored picture that contains no colors. A miracle. In Guadalupe, there is no way out. Here, a divine lady manifested and left behind a material piece of evidence for her existence. By the way, after this apparition, the sexual barriers between the Spanish conquerors and the Indios, the original inhabitants, fell, and a completely new type of human was created. And a total reconciliation was brought about between the warring religions.

The pope is infallible, and this is a dogma of the Catholic Church. True to Jesus's orders to Peter the Apostle, in Heaven "all will be bound which you bind on earth, and all will be dissolved in heaven that you dissolve on earth." The Roman popes see themselves as the direct successors of Peter the Apostle, and logically they can do no wrong in Church matters, because even if they did announce something wrong, it would be blessed in Heaven anyway.

Now, we know from history that the popes were not infallible, even in Church matters. My countryman, Catholic theologian Dr. Hans Küng, has remarked, "The errors of Church teaching are numerous and serious; today, when open discussion can no longer be forbidden, they can no longer be disputed even by conservative theologians and Church leaders."[27] The condemnation of Galilei, who taught that the Earth moved around the Sun, and not the other way around, the condemnation of Darwin's theory of evolution, and the excommunication of the Patriarch of Constantinople were all based on the better-known errors. Not to speak of Catholic birth control. A list of erroneous decisions would be a long one.

Now, the popes believe that they are guided by the Holy
Spirit in their positions as teachers. How come? With all *those*
errors? According to Catholic teaching, the Holy Ghost is equal
to God, as the Father, the Son, and the Holy Spirit are all one.
This would mean that God announces things that are wrong
through the Holy Spirit and its earthly representatives. The
illogic of this bites its own tail. Dr. Hans Küng had his permission to teach religion revoked by the Church due to his critical
questioning. After that, he became Professor for Ecumenical
Theology at the University of Tübingen and was allowed to
think about world ethics. Much the same thing happened
to his contemporary, Eugen Drewermann. This doctor of theology also had his license to teach religion revoked because he
thought aloud—too loudly. Drewermann thought about the
all-merciful, good God and could not stand it any longer:

> *A God who can do everything and still does nothing, deserves
> not to be considered benevolent, if he watches so many disastrous
> things without doing anything. Or the other way around, if he
> were really good and could not himself prevent things, he would
> not be almighty; both characteristics can not be united, as long
> as the world is the way it is, a vale of tears. Both characteristics,
> almightiness as well as goodness, inalienably belong to the con-
> cept of the Divine, according to Christian theology. There can
> be no other conclusion; it is the world itself that contradicts the
> Christian God as its creator. Or to put it another way, the moral
> assertion that is incorporated in the Christian idea of the god-
> head, is rendered ad absurdum by the reality of the world.*[28]

It is not Erich von Däniken who is bringing up these critical and logical questions. Many others have done so, among
them not a few professors of theology, who afterward had to

pick up their hats and leave. The Church will not brook intelligence. Unlike the professors, I do not need to be afraid of losing a teaching position.

The question about *the* Mother of God who appeared in Fátima and elsewhere, and obviously had the power to produce a Sun miracle, has been asked by others too.[29] Who was shown there? Who is influencing humans or at least tries to? Those who have researched this material are certain of the validity of these events, that some of these apparitions really occurred and are not just figments of imagination in a few heads.

Some years ago Dr. Johannes Fiebag, a brilliant thinker, who died far too young and who can be counted alongside people like Hans Küng and Eugen Drewermann, set up a hypothesis to try to explain some of these apparitions—a mimicry hypothesis.[30] In science, *mimicry* is the term used to describe animals' and plants' adaptation to their environment. Mimicry is also part of the protective or camouflaging appearance of butterflies, grasshoppers, or chameleons, who have adapted to their environments so well that their enemies can no longer see them. They take on shapes and colors that make them almost invisible. Nature is full of mimicry. Based on this fact, Dr. Fiebag asked himself whether mimicry was also applicable to extraterrestrials:

> *Don a virtual reality body suit, step into a world created by a programmer out of bits and bytes, take on a shape you fancy, or which you believe the inhabitants of that world might like. Fairy or elf, God or the Devil, spaceship traveler or little gray man. No matter. Let your imagination run riot. Or use the programmed imagination installed for the inhabitants of your artificial world.*

The virtual figures you meet believe in higher beings that appear as flying humans from Magonia? This is no problem. A quick hand movement, you type in an option from the menu provided for you and, hey presto, you are a spaceman from Magonia. You turn up again a few centuries later. (Centuries mean nothing to you who are outside the entire system.) You find out that alien intelligences are thought to be little grey men who whisk through space in shining starships and steal women's babies? No problem. You type in an option from your menu, and you are such a UFOnaut.

Why would you do this? Perhaps it is just a game to you. Perhaps it is a test. Perhaps it is an experiment. Perhaps it is a higher program that you and your colleagues are working on. Perhaps it serves to "lift" the consciousness-contents created in the virtual world, to develop them, to stimulate them to further evolution beyond the phases of regression or standstill.

Naturally, you know that you are not God. You make mistakes. You may have to deceive certain consciousness-contents, which you have developed inside the artificial environment of your computer. They must not realize the truth, whatever that truth may be. Not yet. Everything needs time. You pretend something in front of these "beings." You playact. You tell them stories, best of all, what they want to hear, that you are really a fairy, that you really come from Magonia, that you really do steal embryos. All depending. And you make sure that any kind of pieces of evidence disappear again . . .

UFO apparitions, apparitions of Mary, of Bigfoot, spaceships that dissolve, spaceships that crash, extraterrestrial corpses and semi-earthly fetuses: all this is as real or unreal as our total reality. The Others even proceed very cleverly and with a certain enigmatic sense of humor. They meet our ancestors who think the Others are gods, not only as beings radiant with light, but as astronauts: the Others use spaceships, which can be built nowadays, they use temples as Earthbases, the purpose of which can only now be recognized. They leave behind technical apparatuses and other artefacts, which are destined to experience adventurous sojourns through history. They have buildings erected that turn out to be data carriers of timeless information.[31]

And what is all this for? Fiebag suggests, "We should begin to question again our origins and our concepts of the world. It is a change of angle with which we view things that will lead us to new futures and insights."[32]

Could the mimicry hypothesis provide the solution to all the inexplicable things that happen in the world of religion? Is this hypothesis able to help explain why a certain Joseph Smith (founder of the Mormon religion) sees an apparition of the angel Moroni who dictates the Book of Mormon to him? Do the messages that were received by various religious founders originate in an outer-earthly world? Are dwarves who have supposedly appeared to many a solitary wanderer in the mountains the same as the jinn (spirits) that appear in great numbers in Arabic literature? Are apparitions nothing but manifestations caused by an alien technology streets ahead of ours? Those who would argue that the good Lord or the divine Almighty is behind it all must have a very different concept of God to the one I have. If all those religions, which squabble with each other so self-righteously, are all inspired by the Spirit of God, then this Spirit of God must be playing a moody and unlovely game with us, as millions of people have so far lost their lives and hundreds of thousands have been tortured *because* of this religious self-righteousness. Notable

Christian theologians who have taken a stance against a pseu-do-God have all been chucked out in the name of religion. In the Islamic world, one would not even dare to begin to ask critical questions.

At least 10 percent of all publicly known cases of appari-tions are factual. Fátima with its Sun miracle is one of them. Basically, there are three possibilities to explain it all:

Looked at historically, there is no Mother of God. She was an invention of the early Church. Many pre-Christian reli-gions already had mother goddesses. So no mother goddess can appear. The apparition must have another source.

It is true that the Mother of God is an invention of the early Christian Church, but the popes have allowed this invention to become reality. True to the gospel passage "that which you will bind on earth, will be bound in Heaven, and that which you dissolve on earth shall be dissolved in Heaven" (Matthew 16:19). An invented Mother of God has become a real Mother of God.

Somebody out there is playing with us. The powers of this alien somebody are far beyond any earthly technology (mim-icry hypothesis). Just as they are playing with us, they could destroy us at any time. Then, one needs to ask, who is this universal Player? Is there a hierarchical order among Players, which ensures that underdeveloped civilizations like us are *not* scrapped? And who or what then is the very highest God behind the Players? Even a civilization of spirit beings that we can't really imagine has to have begun sometime.

Variation a) is really quite sensible. The only problem with it is that apparitions of Mary do exist. Variation b) is the least likely. Why? Because Jesus really would have to have been the "only born son of God." But every expert with any number of doctorates, who has dealt with this question in our times and knows how the gospels were compiled, will deny the concept of a son of God.[33, 34, 35] And if the Holy Ghost really was the basis of the gospels, as well as the Koran, how could it then declare, via Mohammed, "But it is not seemly for Allah to have · had a son"? This son of God finally would have been sent to humans to liberate them from original sin. Which then lands us back with the contradictions of the Old Testament.

Variation c) is possible, but there is no real proof to hand. Now I am one of those people who will always ask for the cause of a thing. (Who or what would be the very highest God behind the Players?) Every event is caused by another event. This assumption is no longer valid in the unspeakably difficult field of quantum physics. The causality principle—cause equals effect—has been suspended. Quantum physics lives in a kind of ghost world, in which we ask ourselves where something as strange as information comes from, or where states like consciousness, the imagination, or creativity come from. The imagination in my head does exist, and I know roughly how neurons and their circuits work in my brain. But this does not explain my imagination. If it arises because of quantum-physical effects, these effects cannot be measured and, apart from a theory, I have no proper understanding of it. If the children of Fátima only experienced the events in their heads, then what was the origin of the Sun miracle? And should the Fátima apparition really only be based on quantum-physical effects, how were the "ghosts" behind the quantum physics able precisely to predict one month before the event that a Sun miracle would take place on October 13, 1917?

One feels quite alone in this world and chases from one contradiction to another. The Sun miracle of Fátima on October 13, 1917 was a real event, triggered by a Mother of God who should not exist, historically speaking, and who was confirmed by a religion that alleges it is the only true one, even though other religions make the same claim. Behind all this there is supposed to be some Holy Ghost, which is at the same time God, and guides the popes—who, in turn, have definitely made erroneous announcements.

With all this confusion, variation c) still suits me best. The popes since 1960 have done everything to make variation c) at least thinkable. Remember:

Fátima 1917. Sister Lucia does not neatly write down the third secret of Fátima until 1941, when she hands the envelope over to the Bishop of Leiria, who, in turn, keeps it in his safe for thirteen years before it is sent to the Holy See in Rome. There, the envelope remains lying somewhere for another eighteen months, until Pope John XXIII opens it on August 1, 1959. John XXIII seals the envelope and gives it back to the Holy Office with the command not to make the message public. Six years later, the same thing happens under Paul VI, and, fourteen years after that, again under John Paul II. On July 18, 1981—after the assassination attempt on the pope—the same thing happens a fourth time. All the popes refuse to publish, with the argument that "it concerns our Faith." Eighty-three years after Fátima (on April 19, 2000), the pope sends a high-ranking emissary to the aged nun Lucia to pose some questions regarding the interpretation of the third secret. This means that things were not clear; the Holy Mother must have expressed herself unclearly eighty-three years before. Moreover, the Holy Ghost had not guided the understanding of the nun, when the latter wrote down the message in 1941. In the middle of 2000, the Holy Office suddenly decides to release the text of the secret—and nothing happens. Had *the* text that was released in June 2000, with a long-winded commentary by Cardinal Ratzinger, been identical to the original text, there would have been no reason not to have released it *before.* The version that was released in the summer of 2000 would have been rendered completely absurd by the popes' statements that they could not publish the secret because it pertained to "the Faith" and it would "cause a panic among humans." They are cheating in the Vatican. Originally, Sister Lucia had said that "the lady" requested the secret should be published on October 17, 1960. Later, Lucia explained that not "the lady" but she herself had set the date, "because one would not, as I felt, understand it before 1960." Even if this statement is true—and was not, as I suspect, foisted on the aged nun—the popes would not have understood the message in 1960 either, because they all refused to publish it. I fear that the Vatican has maneuvered itself into a dreadful story from which it cannot disentangle itself. The reasons are compelling:

On October 18, 1942, Pope Pius XII had dedicated Fátima to the "Immaculate Heart of Mary." Pius XII did *not* know the secret! (It was not opened until 1959.) This dedication emphatically advanced Fátima to become a Catholic place of pilgrimage in honor of the Mother of God. This dedication could not be reversed, as the popes are infallible. Fátima grew and grew into an unbelievable center of the Catholic cult of Mary. In 1959, Pope John XXIII read the message for the first time and must have been terribly shocked because no announcement by Mother Mary was contained in it. The same happened to the succeeding popes. Logically, they could no longer make the Fátima message public because Fátima had meanwhile become a unique place of pilgrimage. The statement issued by the popes, that the message had to do with "our Faith," was absolutely correct. The same goes for the statement by John Paul II, who had said in Fulda, in 1980, "My predecessors of the Holy See preferred a diplomatic version because of the serious content." Correct. It *concerned* the Faith in the truest sense of the term and was very "serious," because how could one have explained to believers afterward that it was not about a message from "the dear Mother of Jesus"? This also explains why the Bishop of Leiria kept the message for thirteen years. Naturally, he had read it and could not make much of it. Perhaps he hoped that the Wheel of Time might turn differently in the future, and perhaps the child Lucia had imagined it all back in 1917. (According to the statement made by Sister Lucia, the envelope was to be opened by the Patriarch of Lisbon and/or the Bishop of Leiria.)

And what might have really been contained in the original text of the third secret of Fátima? Nobody knows, apart from those in the know. But 70,000 people witnessed a Sun miracle, a rotating, glowing disc, which appeared for twelve minutes. I consider this to be a good clue that a group of extraterrestrials was concerned. Maybe, in the message, they were greeting humankind and were pointing out that we do not live alone in the universe. Perhaps they even indicated that they would come back soon and that it would be sensible if humankind were prepared for such an event. As long as the Vatican refuses to publish the unvarnished truth, any halfway sensible thought is justified because it certainly did not happen the way the popes and then-Cardinal Ratzinger have depicted it. *Quod erat demonstrandum.*

As popes and members of the Holy Office, generally speaking, do not know much about space travel, and even less about ETs, about interstellar distances or about the multitude of possibilities of extraterrestrial life, much less about technologies of the distant future, one has to fear that they themselves do not understand the "serious" (John Paul II) nature of the message of Fátima. Given their unshakeable faith, they might assume that the message had come from the divine adversary, the Devil. That would have been just as bad as a message from extraterrestrials because, after all, Fátima has become a Catholic place of pilgrimage.

Personally, I dislike the entire development as much as countless believing Catholics do. I myself was brought up as a Catholic. I, too, find it painful to have to say goodbye to the beautiful images from my childhood. I know the wonderful hymns sung in honor of the Mother of God. I know the very pleasant feeling of connection with other believers in a church. I know the Gregorian chants, the organ music, the smell of incense, and the candlelight. If I have brought up the same kinds of questions here that have been raised by eminent theologians, and have offered some possible answers, then one should not start looking for deep psychological reasons for it. I am not conducting a reckoning with something from the past, nor do I wish to confuse believers (who will not be reading this book anyway). So why all these reflections about Fátima and the Old Testament? Because the way the whole thing is portrayed is not the truth. Because people do not like to be lied to. Because other people should also have thoughts about God and their religion and should not just stubbornly believe in something. Belief needs no proof—and makes you happy. That is precisely the danger. Every church and every sect, after all, maintains they are in possession of the lone truth. So people fight for this (alleged) truth and resort to swords and machine guns. And might they not resort to an atomic bomb or a chemical weapon—in God's name—to eradicate those who believe in something different? The number of conflicts worldwide that have a religious background are rising every year. The planet is teeming with pious fanatics and ruthless warriors of God. Good, sensible people behave decently toward other people, whether they are religious or not. To make good, decent people do something terrible and evil, you need religion. Any dreadful deed can be justified in the name of religion. This is the reason I do what I do. I am defending myself against religious righteousness and look upon myself more as a "worker in the vineyard of the Lord," because most of what we humans attach to the good Lord is an insult toward the grandiose creation. The path to enlightenment was always a stony one, and our earthly ideal of morals and ethics need not necessarily be identical with the way otherworldly beings think.

Now that the Mother of God has appeared (not just in Fátima), there is at least a vague way out of the dilemma for believers, and to set the world right to a degree. Let us take variation c), the mimicry hypothesis. Somebody out there is playing with us. This somebody knows human beings and their religions, of course, and knows that millions of us believe absolutely in a Mother of God. So, they slip into the role of this Mother of God, call themselves by that name, and manifest themselves as such. And the world is back on line. Ave Maria!

CHAPTER 3

Entire Forests of Stupas

There is no customs duty on thoughts, but you still
get a lot of hassle.

—KARL KRAUSE

THE ROAD LAY IN semi-darkness. Everywhere the little fires
of hot-food stalls flickered in the gloom. The place was teeming with brown people, all sitting on tiny stools that were only
about 15 centimeters high, and even the little tables seemed
made for dwarfland. Was I among Lilliputians? No, the
people around me were normal sized, although the height
of the tiny stools made their knees come up to their chests.
I actually felt rather lost at the thought of having to sit there
like that, a bit like a giant in kindergarten—and I myself am
only 1.68 meters tall. A wide variety of odors penetrated my

nose, like little flags of different colors, from sweet to sour, rancid to burnt, every imaginable smell.

The next crossroad in this chessboard pattern of the town's streets brought me to the main arterial road. Now all the cooking smells became mingled with the stink of traffic exhaust fumes. Even the edge of the main road was cluttered with hundreds of little tables and stools. In between them, laid out on the ground, were masses of goods: plastic kitsch for the little ones, sandals and shoes beside shirts and bolts of fabrics in all colors, and then, in a line about 60 meters long, a stretch of spectacles, for any face or nose on this Earth. I had trouble trying to avoid treading on anything.

Asia's cities and towns all look the same; they taste alike and, superficially at least, the people seem to be the same too. Yet the town I was walking through was completely different.

Right in front of me, less than 300 meters away in the center of the crossroad, what appeared to be a multiphase space rocket pointed toward the sky. It was illuminated by numerous spotlights and was covered from its base to its tip with pure gold. An extremely awe-inspiring sight. I felt respect in the face of this stupendous accomplishment in the name of religion. What looked like a rocket was just one of several thousand pagodas in a land of golden stupas—bell-shaped structures, each of which ends in a narrow tower. Years ago, the country was called Burma. Today, this country, situated between Thailand, China, and India, is called Myanmar. The city I was exploring is called Yangon (formerly Rangoon). The place is teeming with indescribably splendid pagodas, even in the midst of all the activity of cars, shops, and pedestrians and along the bank of the

Ayeyarwady River. Only the Buddha and the government are wealthy in this country. Nowhere else in the world is the Buddha revered so much as in Myanmar. For millennia, year after year, the believers have sacrificed tons of gold leaf and precious gems to adorn the pagodas and to attain some form of relief in this life or the next. I was standing in front of the Sule Pagoda, which is also called "the Heart of the City." Although night had fallen some time ago, and the traffic all around the pagoda gave rise to a bad smell, here and there I could see believers in front of small shrines, staring reverently at the figures and small lights behind the grids. A kind of enchantment reigns here that the world outside Myanmar cannot comprehend.

The Sule Pagoda in Yangon stands in the middle of the busy traffic.

A golden stupa at the Ayeyarwady River.

This country is interwoven with religion and astrology. The children do not have personal names as we know them, and they do not adopt the names of their fathers. Moreover, one cannot distinguish the sex of a child purely by his or her name. Boys or girls can be called Kyan Kyan, Zan Zan, Maung Maung, or even Cho Cho. The difference between male and female is only apparent later on, when the words *Mr.* or *Mrs.* are added. All names have something to do with the day of the week and the month of birth, but they can be changed during the course of one's life. So, for example, a person may use only the first five letters of a month if they are born on a Monday. Moreover, the glyphs of the alphabet, consisting of thirty-three letters, must be rising or consecutive, as in Tuesday, Wednesday, Thursday. The reason is that life is seen as rising upward. If someone starts a company, the name of that company will be determined by an astrologer. The name of the firm can be altered only by a superior astrologer, for example, if business is not going well. Somebody who was born on a Friday will usually sacrifice at an altar that is dedicated to Friday. It is hardly surprising that, in this country, thousands upon thousands of pagodas are astronomically aligned.

The Sule Pagoda in front of which I was standing was dedicated to the planets, the celestial animals, and the eight celestial directions. Myanmar was a monarchy before the British made it a colony. Reigning King Mindon (1853–1878) transferred his residence to Mandalay, a fairy-tale city in the center of Myanmar, precisely on the 2,400th anniversary of the death day of the Buddha. Even the name Mandalay sounds like music to Western ears. Mandalay was Buddha's city, and in the face of the British threat, King Mindon called "the fifth great synod" in Mandalay, a gathering that was rather similar to the councils in the Christian Church. At that time, in 1872, 2,400 Buddhist scholars came together in Mandalay and compiled the Tipitaka canon, the Buddhist "teaching of the three baskets." Before that, the teaching had existed only in writing on palm leaves, but the king now had it chiseled into 729 marble tablets. They were to remain indestructible until the coming of the next Buddha. According to this teaching, a Buddha will return every 5,000 years. Two thousand four hundred years had passed since the Buddha's last appearance, so the tablets had to last for another 2,600 years. King Mindon therefore had a pagoda erected over each marble tablet. The result was a complex that has been dubbed the "biggest book in the world," and rightly so. A modern paper copy consists of thirty-eight volumes of 400 pages each. Christianity really cannot come up with anything similar to match it.

Considering their weapons technology, it was no wonder that the British were victorious over the kings of Mandalay. They built a fort and ruled over the country and the river right up north to the border with China. Literary chronicler and protagonist of British colonial power Rudyard Kipling made Mandalay immortal in his poem:

> On the road to Mandalay,
> Where the flyin' fishes play . . .
> Come you back to Mandalay,
> Where the old Flotilla lay . . .
> For the wind in the trees
> And the temple bells they say,
> You British soldier,
> Come you back to Mandalay.

—R. KIPLING, "The Road to Mandalay," 1887

The British called Myanmar Burma, but in 1989 the country reverted back to its original name. Like the story of most countries, Myanmar's history begins with a mythological time. Sometime in the past, dragons or flying serpents (*nagas*) came from the sky and had instructed the first human beings.[1] They also showed humans how to extract gold and precious stones from the earth and from water. To this day, the people of Myanmar see the 2,170 kilometer long river Ayeyarwady as the line of the dragon, and even the outline of the country is thought to be like that of a dragon. The Ayeyarwady is like the jugular vein of the country, comparable to the Nile in Egypt.

The dragon motif is known all over Asia and is one of the prehistoric riddles of humankind. No human being can have ever seen a fire-spewing dragon because no such being exists in the evolution of our planet. I once heard that ancient memories of dinosaurs might be the root of the motif, but this comparison does not work either. When dinosaurs were at their peak sixty million years ago, not even a prototype human being existed.

In China, Myanmar's neighbor, dragon kings were the original bringers of culture and the founders of the first dynasty. Several Chinese rulers enjoyed the privilege of experiencing a celestial flight in a flying dragon, together with their entire households.[2] Chinese mythologies feature reports about this celestial dragon, describing how it had flown across the Earth making a loud noise and terrifying everyone, but how it had also brought items of culture to humans and instructed them in many things.[3] During the reign of Chuen, one of the founding emperors of China, the divine architect Yu had an enormous tower erected in the middle of a lake in order to observe more easily the flight movements of the dragon in the sky.[4]

The celestial dragon is universally present in the mythologies—right into Christian times, although a dragon was almost certainly never observed. Saints George, Sylvester, and Michael have always been connected with dragons. Of course, the dragon appears in the Book of Revelation of the New Testament and also among the prophets of the Old Testament. Dragons appear in pictorial form on early Sumerian cylinder seals and on Egyptian palettes; they are depicted as flying serpents in the tombs of pharaohs in the Valley of the Kings. For the (much later) Central American peoples, the feathered serpent was a symbol of gods who had come from above. Just to mention in passing, the same motif—in the form of the thunderbird—appears among North American Indians. No one can deny that the flying serpent has a firm place in many creation myths. Why? Psychologists think our ancestors had observed an unusual bird. But birds do not spew fire, do not make loud noises, do not make the valleys tremble, do not take passengers on board, do not beget children (which happened in China), and certainly do not instruct humans.

People in the Stone Age knew birds and had names for them. But the "thing" that was observed all over the world could not have been a bird. People groped for words and comparisons because this indescribable thing did not exist. At some point, it became a fire-spewing serpent and, in the Asiatic world, a dragon. Shocked by what they had seen, fathers reported these impressive events to their sons and their grandsons. Over the course of time, these original factual accounts lost their contours and finally found a nesting place in myths. A myth is a kind of vague folk memory.

The same happened in Myanmar. No country borders existed in the Stone Age, so what was true for Chinese mythology was equally valid for the (present) neighboring country, Myanmar. The first historically verifiable group of people in the land along the Ayeyarwady River are the Mon people. The Mon came from central Asia, and linguistically, they belonged to the Mon-Khmer culture. This is known from inscriptions. The Mon people had adopted Buddhism and, according to legends, had erected the first pagoda as early as 2,500 years ago: the Shwedagon Pagoda in Rangoon.

The present-day Shwedagon Pagoda is almost indescribable: "It is said that there is more gold on the Shwedagon Pagoda than in the Bank of England." This quote is from the only really outstanding travel guide on Myanmar, by Wilhelm

Klein and Günter Pfannmüller. Both men are extraordinarily knowledgeable about this country:

> *The massive, bell-shaped stupa alone forms a single, 100 m tall treasure chest. If the legend can be believed, eight hairs of the last Buddha, as well as further relics of the three Buddhas who lived before him [who, it is said, came in intervals of 5,000 years], are contained inside. And outside . . . Well, the stupa is bedecked with 8,688 gold plates, of which each individual one would be worth about DM 1,000 [£320 or $490] according to present calculations. 5,448 diamonds, as well as 2,317 rubies, sapphires and topazes adorn its top; a gigantic emerald that catches the first and last sunbeams of the day forms the crown of this structure.[5]*

When I visited the Shwedagon Pagoda, I had trouble separating the past from the present. Occasionally, I felt as if I were in the middle of an unreal science-fiction film. First of all, you have to climb a seemingly endless path from forecourt to forecourt until, finally, after hundreds of steps, you find yourself near the circular, golden center. Here can be found rows of shrines, one next to another. Electronically controlled miniature lamps behind the Buddha-heads allow rings and beams of light to shoot out of the Buddha's brain. Rings and bundles of rays also appear to tear toward the Buddha from outer space. The complete enlightenment. (This may sound sarcastic but is not meant to be.) It is not very different in our Christian places of pilgrimage. The only difference is that you are nearly smothered by the glittering gold and diamonds in the Shwedagon Pagoda. Inadvertently, I was reminded of the Spanish conquistadors, who had set out for Central and South America and murdered the Maya and the Inca for their gold. Thank Heaven the European conquerors knew nothing about the land of gold called Myanmar that had existed for thousands of years. I dare say an incomparable culture would have been destroyed there too in the name of the Cross.

The Shwedagon Pagoda, fully gilded with gold,
is here covered with bamboo mats.

I spent hours strolling through the Shwedagon Pagoda and often found it difficult to tear my gaze away from the figures. There stood the statues, covered in layers of indefinable gold and silver alloys, just as if they had sprung from the *Star Wars* films. Beside them were the mystical helpers, the protectors of the Buddha, which could not have existed in the lifetime of the last Buddha. This is mythology cast in gold and silver, non-rusting for eternity and a unique pictorial lesson. Naturally, the dragon motif is not missing either.

Buddha and his helpers are omnipresent in the pagoda.

The top terrace is covered in white marble slabs. In the middle, the golden stupa rears up with a circumference of 433 meters. The stupa itself lies on an octagonal plate on the ground, with eight smaller stupas standing at each of the eight corners, making a total of sixty-four. In front of these are some fabulous sphinx-like beasts, pure mythology. The stupa, which is about 100 meters tall, rises into the sky like a glowing finger pointing at the universe, surrounded by diamonds shooting colored flashes of light. Right at the top is a small globe of heavy gold with a diameter of 25 centimeters. On the golden globe is a 76 carat emerald, which stores up energy from the first to last sunbeam. Laser technicians would find it quite inspiring.

Our planetary system and the universe are present everywhere in the Shwedagon Pagoda. According to Myanmaran traditions, both the Sun and the Moon are thought of as spheres.[6] This is why there is a solar devotion area, to which are assigned Sunday and the divine bird Garuda. Monday and the tiger are assigned to the lunar devotion space. Every planet has its days and animals. Accordingly, there is a space for the worship of each planet in the Shwedagon Pagoda, as follows:

Mars corresponds with Tuesday. The animal is the lion.
Venus corresponds with Friday. The animal is the guinea pig.
Jupiter corresponds with Thursday. The animal is the rat.
Saturn corresponds with Saturday. The animal is a mythological serpent being (*naga*).
Mercury corresponds with Wednesday. The animal is the elephant.

Then, there are places of worship for the unknown planet, for the eight days of the week, and for the Sakka kings, who originated from the celestial fields of Mount Meru. As all Myanmarans are already connected with the days of the week and with the planets through their personal names, the worshippers will worship at those shrines assigned to them: those called Tuesday at the shrine of Mars, those with a Thursday name at the Jupiter shrine, and so on. Naturally, the Myanmarans also have their own calendar. The week consists of eight days, and the year 1999, when I visited that country, corresponded to the year 1361 in Myanmar.

Just as miracles occur at Christian places of pilgrimage, they happen here too. Certain parts of the Shwedagon Pagoda are specially reserved for miracles. Here, the believers pray particularly fervently and plead for relief in this and the next life. The believers bow in front of the "stone of Fulfilling Wishes," lift up the stone and say, "May this stone become light if my wish is fulfilled." If the stone remains heavy, as it is, the miracle will have to wait, or the wish will remain unfulfilled for reasons of divine providence. Many miracles have occurred in this and other pagodas all over the country. And who is responsible for them? The Great Spirit of the Universe? IT, which is around us and in us, and of which we are a microscopic part? There is even a raised platform in the Shwedagon Pagoda, which is exclusively reserved for men. Here too miracles happen.

It was evening. The gold of the pagoda was glowing a shiny dark yellow. At the top, on the point of the stupa, sparkled the emerald. Suddenly, a team of people turned up on the marble platform, each one carrying a broom. At a command, the team moved slowly around the temple platform, and here and there, a little pile of dirt appeared, which was then removed by a second team with a waste bin. I heard that the ladies and gentlemen did this job voluntarily, but only those whose birthday is on that particular day are allowed to do the work. This is how things work with the Myanmarans. Astrology determines life from birth to the sound of the gong at death, and then on, into the next round.

The daily cleaning team at the Shwedagon Pagoda consists only of people who are celebrating their birthday on that day.

There is a tradition about the original creation of the Shwedagon Pagoda, which goes back much further than Buddhism. But what is this Buddhism really?

In ancient Indian, the word *Buddha* means the "Enlightened One." The Buddha's real name was Siddhartha, which in Sanskrit means "one who has attained his goal." Buddha's birth year is set at approximately 560 BC. He came from the noble family of the Sakajas and grew up in his father's splendid palace in the foothills of the Nepalese Himalayas. In keeping with the custom of Indian noble houses, in which a name from the holy scriptures (the Vedas) is chosen, his personal name was Gotama (Gautama). When he was twenty-nine years old, he found he had had enough of his boring, useless, luxurious life. He left his home, wandered around like a beggar, and practiced meditation for many years. He was seeking a new way to give meaning to life. When exactly this all happened, nobody knows. One day, while he was sitting under a bodhi tree in Bodh Gaya, the universe opened itself to him; the day of enlightenment had arrived. Suddenly, he felt himself to be an incarnation of a celestial being. He began to preach, attracted disciples, and praised the path of enlightenment, which all flesh would have to walk. He founded the order of monks called Sangha, wandered through northern India, and died at the Nepalese border.

Buddha himself—like Jesus—left no writing. His sermons were recorded by his disciples and were spread by them. Buddha taught the "four truths," the path on which every human being could become an enlightened being. In this, Buddha assumed the existence of previous *and* future Buddhas (Enlightened Ones). In his departure speeches, in the *Mahāparinibbāna-Sutta,* he spoke of future Buddhas. One of them, he announced, would appear at a time in which India was overpopulated with human beings. The villages and towns would be as densely inhabited as chicken runs. There would be 84,000 towns in the whole of India. A king called Sankha would live in the city Ketumati (present-day Benares), and he would rule the whole world, not with violence but with justice. Under his rule, the exalted Metteya (also called Maitreya) would appear on Earth. Metteya would be an extraordinary and unique "chariot driver and knower of the world," a teacher of gods and humans, the Perfect Buddha in fact.

In contrast to Christianity, according to which the religious founder was made into a god, Buddha is not a deity. The believers do not pray to him directly, but they wish to attain enlightenment and help via Buddha's teaching and spirit. During the course of 2,500 years, the most diverse Buddhist schools have arisen. Each school refers back to traditions of the original Buddha's disciples and to knowledge arrived at through enlightenment. But they are all agreed on the main points.

The Buddhist Myanmarans believe the holy Mount Meru is situated at the center of the world. Seven seas surround it, and there, various different levels of being are to be found. There is, for example, a kingdom of the senses, a realm of shapelessness, and a realm of the finest matter. In total, thirty-one levels of being exist that lead far beyond Mount Meru and into the universe. Out there, innumerable worlds and heavens exist, which are supposed to be far distant from each other. Even the galaxies come and go. At present, there are supposed to be 10,100,000 universes like ours, in which there is life of all kinds.

According to Buddhist ideas in Myanmar, a new Buddha will appear every 5,000 years. The legend of the Shwedagon Pagoda says that the hill on which this shrine was later built had been a holy place for a long time before, as relics of an *even earlier* Buddha had been preserved here. These relics consisted of an article of clothing, a ladle, and a staff. Five thousand years had passed, and a king called Okkapala was now waiting for the new Buddha. This was at a time when the present Buddha was still a youth living in the luxury palace of his parents. The millennium had almost passed when the present Buddha had his moment of enlightenment under the bodhi tree in Bodh Gaya and appeared to King Okkapala in the precise spot in Myanmar where the Shwedagon Pagoda stands today.

Whereas Christianity has its church towers and steeples and Islam its minarets, Buddhism has its stupas. A stupa has many meanings for a Buddhist; it can be seen as a symbol for the end of life's journey; it may be a tomb, or the center of creative power. With its division into three parts, the stupa mirrors the tripartite nature of Buddhism, through the base, the dome, and the tower. The number three in Buddhism is looked upon as the characteristic dimensions of space. The stupa is also seen as the "means of traveling to the world of the gods," which is why a Buddha performing ritual hand movements sits inside so many stupas. Originally, the stupa is only supposed to have had the shape of half an egg with a mast on top. The great teachers or masters came out of the egg, but the stupa is also a symbol of the cosmos, and its shape symbolizes the world mountain Meru. As an old globetrotter and worker "in the vineyard of the Lord," I was at once alerted to a parallel in a continent not so far removed, while studying the stupas. A short detour will presently bring me back to the stupas.

South America: in the Sierra Nevada of Santa Marta in Colombia, there once lived the tribe of the Kogi (or Kagaba) Indians, who were almost exterminated by the Spaniards in the sixteenth century. Only a few survived. Their towns, which had meanwhile become totally overgrown by the jungle, were not rediscovered again until the twentieth century, when they were partially excavated.

The first European researcher to make an effort to find out more about the Kogi Indians was the Austrian professor Theodor Preuss.[7] Preuss found out that the Kogi ascribed the creation to a great original mother called Gauteovan. She was the ancestor of the four original priests, the progenitors of the priestly house. The home of these original priests was somewhere in outer space, and their laws arrived with the Kogi "from outside." When the original priests came to Earth, they wore masks, which they did not take off until much later. The priests passed on their office to their sons. They were educated in temples for a novice period lasting nine years, so that the knowledge of the fathers could be passed on from one generation to the next without being influenced. This education took place in nine years of darkness.

Kogi mythology tells of battles with four original priests against demons and animals. Lightning bolts were hurled, there was a lot of flying about in all directions, and the seeds of various plants were brought to Earth. Masks were worn by the gods, one of which was hidden inside a hill or mountain. A long time passed; the Earth brought forth humans with unnatural tendencies, who used all species of animals for sexual intercourse. The top chieftain had thereupon opened the portals of Heaven and allowed it to rain for four years. The priests had built a magic ship and gathered all species of animals and birds, and also plants and seeds, inside it. For four long years there was red and blue rain, and all over the world huge lakes were created. Finally, the magic ship had become stranded on the crest of the Sierra Negra (which is the name it still had in the Kogi legend). "Now all the evil ones had been destroyed, and the priests, the older brothers, *all came down from Heaven*, whereupon Mulkueikai [a priest] opened the door and placed all the birds and four-footed creatures, all the trees and plants on Earth. This was performed by all the divine persons called Father Kalgusiza. They left behind a monument in memory of this in all the temples."[8]

This is strange. The Kogi legends speak of sodomy. This also happened in Genesis, chapter 19, before the destruction of Sodom and Gomorrah. "All came down from Heaven" we are told by the Kogi myth. The Sumerian king list says, "After the Flood had passed, kingship once more descended from Heaven." And if anybody were now to believe that the Spaniards had brought this knowledge to Colombia, he or she would be very mistaken, as the Kogi myth existed long before the Spaniards came, and the Sumerian king list was not discovered until the nineteenth century. So what has any of this to do with the stupas in Asia?

Dr. Gerardo Reichel-Dolmatoff was the most knowledgeable expert on the Kogi culture, which he studied for many years. Reichel-Dolmatoff discovered that all the Kogi structures had the shape of stupas and can only be understood in connection with events in space.[9] The Kogis perceived the cosmos as an egg-shaped space determined by seven points: north, south, east, west, the zenith, the nadir (opposite the zenith), and the center. Within the space defined in this way, there are nine levels—nine worlds—of which the middle one, the fifth, is represented by our world. All Kogi houses are built according to this pattern. All of them are at the same time models of the Kogi cosmos.

Four levels lie below the surface of the Earth, humans exist on the fifth, and a further four lie above. This produces the shape of an egg, in which the four levels above humans are formed by the stupa. A mighty post protrudes through the roof of the stupa of the men's house, like a flag pole aimed at the sky. Diagonally opposite is the women's house with two cross-beams protruding from the stupa roof. Year after year, on March 21 (at the beginning of spring) the post on the roof of the men's house throws a long shadow into the shadow of the crossed beams of the women's house. The two shadows become one. The phallus penetrates the vagina, a symbol of spring, and the seed is to be sown in the earth.

All the Kogi structures lay in terraces above each other like the pagodas in Myanmar. The largest Kogi town that I visited around forty years ago is called Burritaca.[10] Admittedly, I have not so far discovered any connection between the structures and the knowledge of the Kogi in Colombia and that of the early peoples in Asia, but the line is evident.

The Kogi town of Burritaca (Colombia) was built like
a wedding cake, with one terrace above the other.

Straw huts like stupas once stood on the topmost terrace at Burritaca.

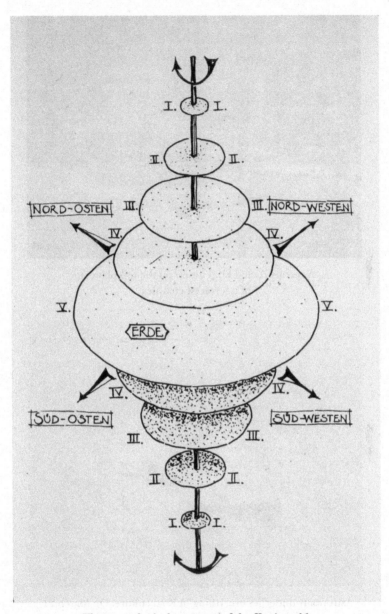

The cosmological structure of the Kogi world.

A reconstructed Kogi house on the top platform
of a terraced complex.

Astronomy underlies everything in Kogi culture. On March 21,
the shadows of the posts on the men's and women's houses unite.

The bell-shape of the stupas is much older than the current era of Buddhism. It can come as little surprise, then, to

hear that, according to Buddhist traditions, several Buddhas were on Earth before the last Buddha. After all, a new one is supposed to grace us with his presence every 5,000 years. Centuries before the enlightenment of the last Buddha, the Jainist religion prevailed in the entire Indian subcontinent. Followers of Jainism maintain in their texts that the foundation of their religion dates back to a time several hundreds of thousands of years ago and that their knowledge originally came from divine beings. (I have discussed this in a previous book.[11])

What is left is the stupa, a bell-shaped structure striving toward the sky, which existed long before the present Buddhism. And Myanmar is the culmination point for all the stupas, a land with "entire forests of stupas." Just in the vicinity of Bagan, a town on the Ayeyarwady, there are more than 2,000 of them. Often, they are found standing densely packed together, in different sizes. Some are more than 2,000 years old. Some of the smaller ones look old and are beginning to decay; others originated in the previous centuries and are constantly being renovated. Over about 200 years, from 1075 to 1287, some 13,000 temples, pagodas, and stupas were erected in the plain of Bagan. "Nowhere else is there such an impressive view, as that of the sight of the Plain of Bagan—one brick-red pagoda next to the other, occasionally with a white top, which rear up to the sky out of the hazy distance on the banks of the greatest river of Myanmar."[12]

On the way to the most splendid structures of Bagan, the Ananda Temple and the Shwesandaw Pagoda, I came past some market stalls, where I kept noticing round cake tins filled with folded-up green leaves. The indigenous population stuffed the leaves into their mouths and then spat out a red liquid. What were they chewing? My first thought was that it was kat, a drug that is mainly consumed in Yemen. Then I also remembered the coca leaves in Peru and Ecuador. In fact, the folded-up green leaves that grow on the areca palm were the national drug of the Myanmarans. Their land is where the betel nut thrives—a small palm nut with a very hard shell, comparable to a nutmeg, and which looks very similar inside. The Myanmarans chop up the nuts, lay them on the betel leaves, which look very much like the leaves of the pepper plant, and then smear on lime and various spices. The whole thing is folded into a little package and shoved straight into one's mouth. The tanning substances in the leaves stimulate a strong production of saliva, which is then colored red by the betel nuts. I tried it but soon spat out the red juice.

Betel nuts lying among leaves. The Myanmarans mix the nuts
with spices and chew them raw. (See also page 156.)

As at the Shwedagon Pagoda in Yangon, in the Ananda
Temple in Bagan, there are many steps, which lead up to the
top. The original structure was built by the Mon people and
was finished in the year 1091, on holy ground, which is of
special importance according to the myths. How could it be
any other way?

The *Glass Palace Chronicle of the Kings of Burma* is a historical-
mythological history written down in the century before last.
According to this chronicle, eight monks appeared one day in
front of the palace of King Kyanzitthas. The monks reported
to the king that they had come from a distant country and had
once lived in the Nandamula Cave. This cave had been inhabited by an earlier Buddha. The king asked the monks to show
him the holy cave. Using the powers of meditation, the monks
made the enchanted landscape appear in front of the eyes of
the king, together with the Nandamula Cave. The king decided

to build in Myanmar a replica of the holy grotto that was some-where in the snow-bedecked Himalayas.

Today the Ananda Temple lies above this cave. To demon-strate the infinite nature of Time, the four tall, golden Buddha statues in the Ananda Temple represent the four last Buddhas of the world ages: Kakusandha, Konagamana, Kassapa, and Gautama. When the statues are observed from a distance, one of them seems to be smiling silently to itself, but it appears to take on a serious expression as soon as one approaches. Very cleverly contrived. The temple itself is an unbelievable object of sheer splendor created by a master architect, and it has a giant stupa at its center. The Buddha is present in a thousand depic-tions, along with images of the timeless ghosts and demons from the pre-Buddhist period. Also in evidence are planet sym-bols and planet altars of Myanmaran astrology. Whenever there is a light mist near the ground, or a hazy light, the central stupa rears its high mast into the sky, just as a Kogi house in distant Colombia rears above the leafy roof of the jungle.

In Bagan, the pagoda cosmos with its eternal circular movements is always present. Every pagoda points to differ-ent key points of mythology, which are not just myths for the pious Myanmaran, but represent a distant reality. Here we have ancient memories of something that the Western world does not understand, depicted in stone. Wherever a visitor goes, he or she will come across these impossible depictions—but in one's imagination and in the distant past nothing is impossible.

Several hairs of the Buddha are preserved as relics in the Shwesandaw Pagoda. The pagoda has the epithet Ganesh, actually a reference to the Hindu elephant god. What does he have to do with the Buddha? As Buddhism is timeless, the Hindu god figures are enmeshed with Buddhism. In Hinduism, Ganesha was one of the five foremost gods, a son of the god Shiva. He was the one who removed all obstacles on Earth. The word *ganesha* is a composite Sanskrit word. *Ganas* are "the hosts," *isa* is the "Lord." So, logically, this means "Lord of the hosts." He is considered to be the mediator between humans and the Almighty. In Hinduism, one believes that Ganesha was not born of his parents Shiva and Parvati, but was created as a brain. The divine beings had consulted before visiting Earth about how they could get rid of obstacles on the new planet. Then, Shiva and Parvati thought of a being with a human body and an elephant's head that could look in all directions and could manipulate things with its hands, feet, and trunk. This offspring of the gods, which is often depicted with a halo, was a synthetic product, created from a genetic design.

In 1955, all the names and characteristics attributed to Ganesha were compiled in a dissertation.[13] Guide, obstacle remover, giver of success, he with the pot-belly, he with the winding trunk, and so on. Like a robot, he is posted in front of doors and entrances, where he will confront anyone who has been forbidden to enter. In India, you meet him everywhere you go. If a Hindu builds a house, he or she first places a Ganesha picture on the building site; Ganesha is meant to remove any expected obstacles. If a Hindu writes a book, he or she first hails Ganesha. Hello, Ganesha! Welcome! Ganesha is also prayed to at the beginning of a journey and is therefore placed at the entrance to Indian railway stations.

So everything has its order, all is neat and tidy. And nobody notices that ancient wisdom is at the root of it all, misunderstood for thousands of years, yet it has survived through religion.

Myanmar was closed to tourism until the last few decades, when the military government needed foreign currency and opened up the country. Today, there is an organized tourist industry, and there are hotels of all categories. A luxury ship with air-conditioned cabins and sumptuous buffets floats on the Ayeyarwady River, which must seem like a space ship from another world to the simple inhabitants along the river. The ship is called the "Road to Mandalay" and always begins its journey of several days on a Sunday, the day of the Sun, dedicated to the divine bird Garuda.

Everywhere in Myanmar, one comes across freshly bathed monks and youths in red-and-orange robes, as every Buddhist in Myanmar has to serve for a period in a monastery. One gets the impression that people here do not walk normally—they seem to float. The upper part of the body is almost motionless, making the people seem as though they are moving along on rollers; this is particularly true of the graceful women who carry heavy loads on their heads. And every morning the cars are adorned with flowers, for their scent.

The pagoda and stupa cosmos haunts the whole country. On Sundays, Garuda reigns—the king of birds, according to the Indian traditions. He is depicted with the wings and beak of an eagle, and sometimes has a dragon's face and a human body. He serves the god Vishnu as a mount and has many notable features. Garuda was highly intelligent, he acted independently, and even won battles alone. The names of his parents are also known: they were called Kasyata and Vinata. Once, Mother Vinata laid an egg, out of which Garuda hatched. It all began normally, or so it seems.

Garuda is the riding animal of the god Vishnu.

Garuda's face was white, his body was red, and his wings were gold colored. He would have cut a dash in any ornithological work. But when Garuda lifted his wings, the Earth shook. He also undertook journeys into space. Moreover, he hated serpents. But he had some good reasons for this last little quirk.

His mother Vinata had been kept captive by serpents after having lost a bet. The serpents promised to release Mummy if her son would fetch them a dish full of the food of the gods, which makes one immortal. The crafty Garuda left no stone unturned to fulfill this condition, but annoyingly the food of the gods that made one immortal could be obtained only from the middle of a sea of flame. At this, the clever Garuda filled up his golden body to bursting with water, which he had sucked up out of the nearby rivers. Then he doused the sea of flames. But—oh horror—the divine mountain teemed with even more serpents, which all spat fire. Then Garuda whirled up clouds of dust, causing the serpents to lose their bearings. Finally, he threw "divine eggs" among the nest of serpents and tore them into a thousand pieces. Some of them, who came too close to him, had their tongues slit. Understandable.

Immediately after his mother was released, Garuda took off for the Moon. But the Moon was in the possession of foreign gods who would not give him permission to land. They shot off flaming arrows at Garuda, but he was immune to them. Garuda's body was invulnerable. When the Moon gods realized this fact, they offered a compromise. Garuda was to receive immortality and become the mount of the god Vishnu. Since then, Vishnu (Sanskrit: the good, the gentle) haunts the universe with the immortal and invincible Garuda.

Just a silly, unimportant story? The tale is very old and contains some really quite Utopian elements: invulnerability, bomb attacks, a flight to the Moon, even the god Vishnu himself requires a space vehicle. In Myanmar, children are taught these stories—not as pretty fairy tales, but as part of a not-understood truth that once happened somewhere at some time. All these stories belong to religion. Even the origins of our word *religion* are disputed. It can be derived from the Latin *relegere* (to observe carefully) or from *religare* (to be connected to God). Religion is supposed to preserve that which is old. This is what happens in Buddhism and Hinduism. The intent is "carefully to observe something connected to God" and preserve it, even if one does not understand it.

One can demonstrate that these religious stories have been eternalized in temples and figures. It is, of course, no different in the Western world, even though we may dispute it. Whoever has visited one of the beautiful Gothic or Baroque cathedrals will know what I mean. There we find splendid depictions of Saint Michael fighting a dragon; representations of saints ascending to Heaven; of youths sitting in fiery furnaces without being harmed; of Moses speaking to a burning bush; of animals reverently listening to Saint Anthony; of angels flying from Heaven to Earth and back again; of flaming swords being manipulated by angels; of objects shooting out beams of light (the ark of the covenant; monstrances); of a Devil with horns and a glowing trident; of Jesus walking on water; and of heavenly hosts, who live in space. We maintain that this is all more or less an artistic depiction of things that were once thought to be truth. Buddhists and Hindus think nothing different. The firm belief in these former truths is not only represented in the cultural field of a religion; it may also contain ancient *knowledge* (in contrast to belief). One example of this is given in Peter Fiebag's book, *Geheimnisse der Naturvölker* (*Secrets of Native Peoples*).

Fiebag, who was a secondary school teacher, was also a traveler and researcher, a globetrotter and writer. Some years ago, he visited the island of Sulawesi (Indonesia) and went to the highlands inhabited by the tribe of the Toraja. There, he soon discovered that the Toraja people look upon themselves as "children of the stars." Attentively, Fiebag began to study the unbelievable traditions of this tribe. The Toraja assured him that their ancient ancestors had come from outer space in the dim and distant past. They still manifest these beliefs to this day—in their religion, in certain words, and even in their homes. The Toraja call their religion *manurun di langi*— "that which came down from Heaven" or "it came down from Heaven." Even the shapes of their houses are supposed to resemble the objects with which the ancient ancestors came from the universe. Fiebag describes:

> *The house is interpreted cosmologically and is not sung about as a ship. The roof of the house is associated with a bird and with flying. Symbolically it stands for space, outer space. A "katik," a long-necked heavenly bird from Toraja mythology, is sticking out of the buffalo's head above the entrance area; this confirms the symbolic expression. The sun wheel is a further symbol of space, just as is the cockerel in the gable area, whose head is associated with the constellation of the Pleiades and whose body is connected with Orion and Sirius . . . A student of languages and native of Toraja, Armin Achsin, has formulated it thus: "The Tongkonan house symbolizes the universe. The roof represents the sky and is connected in the mind with the universe. The central pillar . . . connects the earth and the sky."[14]*

The Kogi Indians in Colombia send their regards.

The houses of the Toraja people on Sulawesi are modeled on the celestial ships of their great teachers.

Fiebag heard that the original ancestor of the Toraja, Tamboro-langi, had reached Earth in a "structure made of iron," a "house that swung down." He found a wife, and several times switched his residence between the Earth and his heavenly home. One day, he became furious and destroyed the "heavenly stair." "As he wished to visit the Earth once more, he came flying to Earth with his heavenly house from the stars. He landed on the mountains of Ullin, in Tana-Toraja, not far from Rantepao. In this way, the Toraja houses were replicas of a star ship that Tamboro-langi once brought to Earth from the Pleiades."[15] This is not just a fairy tale–like story, but knowledge possessed by a tribe still living to this day. It is demonstrated in their names and buildings.

Houses in the heavens? Nothing but fantastic embroidery? I would recommend to any tourist traveling to Thailand, for whatever reasons, to visit the publicly accessible parts of the royal palace in Bangkok. You can see images of the history of the Thai monarchy in a wonderful picture gallery there. You will find pictures of entire houses and palaces that fly through the clouds. In the Temple of the Emerald Buddha, you will see a pictorial representation of the Ramakian. The Ramakian is the Thai version of the Indian Ramayana epic. Stories from the Ramayana are illustrated in full color on 178 sections. The observer will see gods with unearthly weapons depicted there. Not a few of the divine figures are moving about in the air and are firing their death-dealing ray-guns from the clouds.

Images of flying palaces and warriors from the
royal palace at Bangkok.

The gods of the Asiatic world employed terrible weapons. Some of them are known today; others are in a Utopian realm even for us. I shall examine this subject further in the next chapter.

CHAPTER 4

Weapons of the Gods

He who insists on his rank has already lost it.
—MAX RYCHNER

CAN YOU IMAGINE A weapon that returns to the attacker like a boomerang but consists of a gleaming flame? A weapon that evaporates waters and envelops the entire planet in water vapor? A weapon that will instantaneously put an enemy army to sleep? A weapon that will create "illusions" so that the enemy attacks and shoots at something that does not exist? A weapon that is capable of tearing apart an entire planet? A weapon that makes the attacker, together with its technology, quite invisible? A weapon that can be deployed from outer space to burn up entire countries? Can you imagine habitats in space that are so vast that thousands of people can live in them? Habitats with their own gardens, fields, running water, and all kinds of facilities that function according to some anti-gravitation principle and can attain unbelievable speeds of travel?

Can you imagine such futuristic things? Perhaps in a thousand years' time? Well now, all these things and more have already existed: this we know—*if* we care to. Where? In ancient Indian literature. For hundreds of years, really since Western powers took over India, we have looked on the ancient Indian traditions with a snooty attitude as something airy-fairy derived from the imagination. Clever scholars have translated the great Indian epics into English and French, always with an arrogant attitude according to which no science exists outside the Western kind. As usual—and I am fed up with writing about it—psychologists and theologians have pounced on the old texts and falsified and twisted just about everything—not out of bad intentions, but out of lack of understanding. The time was not yet ripe.

Times have changed. The Indian Sanskrit scholars have awoken from their "Sleeping Beauty" sleep and have begun to examine their own epics, vedas, and ancient texts under a magnifying glass, so to speak; they are looking at them armed with the knowledge of our times. Ever more texts were added, the mountain of information has grown, and the Western experts on Indian studies are meanwhile looking on aghast. In ancient India, they were not creating science-fiction stories, not speculating on fabulous weapons, not imagining spaceships—all of this was once a reality. We can no longer avoid this realization, and those India experts who still do not understand should leave their teaching positions.

Let us start with some simple things. In the Vymaanika-Shaastra, an ancient collection of different texts, the following technologies are described:

- a type of mirror that can be used to attract or draw in energy;
- a device that allows a flying vehicle to be enlarged or reduced at will during flight;
- a device for storing radiating energy;
- an instrument that can measure the intensity of lightning;
- an apparatus for prospecting the most diverse natural resources under the surface of the planet (minerals, ores, gold, and so on);
- a device that can turn bright daylight into darkness;
- a device that can neutralize wind pressure;
- a sonic canon;
- twelve different types of electricity;
- an apparatus that can be used to capture pictures and conversations from flying enemy vehicles;
- a machine that can tap solar energy;
- an apparatus to stop the movement of an enemy flying machine;
- a gadget that can make one's own flying vehicle invisible;
- crystals that produce energy;
- an apparatus that repulses chemical and biological substances used as weapons;
- a protective shield around one's own machine;
- several types of metal that repulse heat;
- motors for flying machines, the energy for which is derived from quicksilver (mercury);
- indescribable alloys that we do not understand yet, because the Sanskrit words are untranslatable.[1]

Sanskrit scholar Dr. Dileep Kumar Kanjilal cites the following old sources that report on terrible weapons, various kinds of flying vehicles and spaceships:

- The Vymaanika-Shaastra
- The Samarangana Sutradhara
- The Yuktikalpataru
- The Mayamatam
- The Ayurveda Rigveda
- The Mahabharata
- The Ramayana
- The Puranas
- The Bhagavata
- The Raghuvamsam
- The Abimaraka of Bhsa
- The Jatakas
- The Avadana literature
- The Kathasaritsagara
- The Yuktikalpataru of Bhoja[2]

These words are only understood by Sanskrit scholars, but they of all people should know where to find the texts about futuristic visions in the deep past. The first translations of texts describing unbelievable events appeared in India in 1968 under the editorship of Swami Brahamuni Parivrajaha, followed in 1973 by the next publication by the Academy of Sanskrit Research in Mysore. This Mysore edition of the Vymaanika-Shaastra contains a running English translation but no commentary. The Hindi edition, on the other hand, contains an introduction, which tells us that the original of the Vymaanika-Shaastra had been found as early as 1918 in the Baroda Royal Sanskrit Library. (A copy of this text that was photographed and dated August 19, 1919, is kept in Poona College. Keyword: Venkatachalam Sarma.)

Chapter XXXI of the Samarangana Sutradhara contains many details about the construction of flying machines. Even if some of these works have only appeared in our times, without exception they all refer back to very ancient Indian texts. The Hindi edition of the Vymaanika-Shaastra refers to ninety-seven old Indian texts that deal with flying apparatuses; the Yuktikalpataru of Bhoja mentions flying vehicles in verses 48 to 50. The oldest translation originates from 1870, when the Western world had no idea of airplanes, let alone spaceships.

The first reference to flying apparatuses, which fly through space with living people on board—and also with gods—appears in the hymns to the Asvinas twins and the demi-gods Rbhus. This is in the Rigveda. The Vedas (ancient Indian *veda*—knowledge) comprise the oldest religious literature of the Indians. Ancient Indian, a language in which the Vedas are compiled, is considerably older than the later Sanskrit literature. The Vedas are a collection of old scriptures that were considered to be "superhuman" and inspired. There are a total of four great blocks of the Vedas. The 1,028 hymns of the Rigveda are addressed to individual gods. Then there is the old Indian national epic, the Mahabharata, with approximately 160,000 verses. It is probably the most voluminous poem of any people. The Ramayana consists of another 24,000 shlokas (an Indian rhyme meter consisting of double lines of verse). Last but not least, there are the Puranas. I will list them here at this point so that the layperson may appreciate the sheer volume of this unbelievable mass of literature at our disposal:

- Vishnu Purana, 23,000 verses
- Naradiya Purana, 25,000 verses
- Padma Purana, 55,000 verses
- Garuda Purana, 19,000 verses
- Varaha Purana, 18,000 verses
- Bhagavata Purana, 18,000 verses
- Brahmanda Purana, 12,000 verses
- Brahmavaivarta Purana, 18,000 verses
- Markandeya Purana, 9,000 verses
- Bhavisya Purana, 14,500 verses
- Vamana Purana, 10,000 verses
- Brahma Purana, 10,000 verses
- Matsya Purana, 14,000 verses
- Kurma Purana, 17,000 verses
- Linga Purana, 10,000 verses
- Shiva Purana, 24,000 verses
- Skanda Purana, 81,000 verses
- Agni Purana, 15,400 verses

If one adds the Mahabharata and the Ramayana to these, we have a total of 560,000 verses! Yes, the ancient Indian literature is voluminous. No other people in the world possesses such mighty traditions; compared with this great torrent of information, our Old Testament dwindles to a mere trickle. Now, these ancient Indian texts were always there, even if they were partly hidden away in monasteries and cellars. But why has it taken until now to search these texts for flying devices and spaceships?

The translators in the nineteenth and twentieth centuries were befogged with the spirit of their own times. If the

Ramayana, for example, spoke of a flying chariot "that made the mountains tremble, took off with a noise like thunder, and burnt forests, meadows and the tops of buildings," the translator would insert the following type of comment: "There can be no doubt that this can only refer to a tropical storm."[3] The scholar of 1884 could not make sense of it in any other way; his was an orderly world. Annoyingly, this attitude haunts the entire Western literature that deals with ancient India. Atrocious! German Professor Hermann Jacobi translated the Ramayana in 1893. He did not do this tidily, verse by verse, but simply left out entire complexes that he considered to be superfluous. Full of arrogance, he annotated passages with comments like "meaningless chatter" or "this passage can be left out, as it contains sheer fantasy."[4]

Searching in the excellent collections of the Bern City and University Library, I found countless volumes about ancient Indian literature, about Indian mysticism, about Indian mythology, and reams of commentaries about the Mahabharata, the Ramayana, and the Vedas. But there were no direct translations. It was extremely frustrating. All the clever brains that had ever written anything about ancient India in German must have been alpha males: you shall not think differently from me. They had been lulled in their own *zeitgeist* that kept them happy; they suffered from professional blindness and had been "vaccinated" with the Bible. The only thing left for me was to stick with the great English-language translations, the translation of the Mahabharata by Potrap Chandra Roy (Calcutta, 1896)[5] and the Ramayana translation by M. Nath Dutt (Calcutta, 1891).[6] The other literature I used will be marked and listed in the Notes at the end of the book.

I have, so far, found only two works in the German-speaking world that have dared to look at the ancient Indian texts with modern eyes. These are the outstandingly researched volume by India expert Lutz Gentes called *Die Wirklichkeit der Götter* (*The Reality of the Gods*),[7] and a modern interpretation of the Vedic texts in the book *Gott and Götter* (*God and the Gods*), by India expert Armin Risi.[8]

The principles of the construction of flying machines are explained in 230 lines in the Samarangana Sutradhara of Bhoja. They are described as being unusually maneuverable, rather like our helicopters. They can hover on the spot in the air, fly round the Earth or beyond. The descriptions are insufficient to reconstruct a copy of the vehicle now, but there was methodology in them, even then. The unknown author remarked, thousands of years ago, that he was not doing this out of lack of knowledge, but to avoid misuse.

Mastery of air and space was not just restricted to the chosen few in those days. We read:

> *The body must be constructed so that it is strong and durable . . . Out of lightweight metal [mica is mentioned, EvD] . . . The power residing in mercury, which is set in motion by the driving force of the whirlwind, enables a human being to travel great distances in the heavens in a wonderful manner. Likewise, a vimana [ancient Indian name for a flying vehicle] can be constructed, so it is as large as the temple for the "God-in-motion." Four strong containers for mercury must be built in. When the latter are heated up by regulated fire in the iron containers, the vimana will develop the power of thunder through the mercury, and it will soon appear like a pearl in the sky.[9]*

In the Vishnu Purana we read:

While Kalki was still speaking, two chariots came down from Heaven before them, which shone like the sun, consisted of precious gems of all kinds, and that moved by themselves and were protected by shining weapons.[10]

King Rumanvat even had a vimana the size of a jumbo jet at his disposal:

Both the King and the harem personnel, but also the group of dignitaries from each part of the city, sat down in the celestial vehicle. They reached the great expanse of the sky and followed the routes of the winds. The celestial vehicle flew across the Earth, over the oceans, and was then steered towards the city of Avantis, where a festival was being celebrated. The vimana stopped, so that the King could take part in the festivities. After a short intermediate stop, the King set off again watched by countless curious onlookers who admired the celestial vehicle.[11]

The hymns of the Rigveda, where they speak about the vimana of the two Asvinas brothers, give details about the flying vehicle. It was triangular, large, and had three levels (*trvrt*) and was flown by three pilots (*tri bandhura*). It had retractable wheels and was built out of light metal that looked like gold. The fuel for this flying vehicle consisted of liquids, called *madhu* and *anna*; no Sanskrit scholars know how to translate these words. The vimana moved more lightly than a bird and was able to fly to the Moon and back with ease. When landing on the Earth, it would make a great noise. The Rigveda explicitly mentions different types of fuel that were kept in varied containers. Every time the vehicle came down out of the clouds, great crowds gathered to watch the spectacle. This vehicle that was capable of space travel carried a total of eight persons. Not bad.

Three flying vehicles are mentioned in section 1.46.4 of the Rigveda. They are all capable of conducting liberation operations from the air. At least one of these vimanas also had amphibian features, as it was able to move about in water as easily as in the air. There is mention of thirty rescue operations that were conducted—rescues from the sea, from caves, and even from torture chambers.

Rigveda sections 1.166.4 to 5.9 describe how buildings shook, trees were uprooted, and how the echo of the noise at take-off was thrown back by the hills when the celestial ship lifted off. Not much different from today. In the entire classical and purana literature of ancient India, the word *vimana* refers to a flying vehicle that shines in the heavens (not that ominous Heaven!) and contains liquid substances for fuel.

In spite of these very clear texts, thousands of years old, European India experts still behave as though all this did not exist, as though the texts were simply fiction, though perhaps woven around a possibly true kernel. The experts believe this kernel to center around a quarrel between two families. These families may have existed, but this does not explain the terrible weapons, nor the vimanas, let alone the cities in space.

The basis for the Mahabharata (the most voluminous of the ancient Indian epics) is the battle between two royal houses. The house of the Kurus is said to have been generated from a king of the Moon dynasty and produced two brothers, the older Dhritarashtra and the younger Pandu. Pandu, the younger, had the throne because his older brother was blind. But the blind brother had still managed to beget one hundred sons: the Kauravas. Pandu, the younger one, had only five sons, the Pandavas. Fate decreed that Pandu was to die while his sons were still minors. No wonder, then, that the Kauravas contrived in various devious ways to get rid of the young Pandavas. When their efforts failed, they had to give their cousins at least some parts of the kingdom. This is how the family drama began.

The Kauravas, way in the majority, challenged the Pandavas to a game of dice. The Panadavas lost and were forced to hand over part of their kingdom and disappear into exile for thirteen years. Inevitably, the Pandavas demanded their kingdom back after the thirteen-year period of exile was over. But the Kauravas, who had meanwhile become very powerful, refused. This was the beginning of the most terrible war ever described in ancient literature. The Mahabharata even tells us that all peoples on Earth had sided with either one or the other of the warring parties. The last battle took place on the field of Kurukshetra and was conducted with extraordinary persistence. Terrible "weapons of the gods" were employed, which the humans had no way of counteracting. The glorious, mighty warriors fell, one after the other. The Pandavas did not win until the eighteenth day, with eighteen of the "great units" of the army being massacred. According to modern calculations, this would have been about four million people. In the end, out of the mighty mass of warriors who had taken part in the battle, just six people remained alive of those fighting on the side of the Pandavas, among them the five sons of Pandu. Of the Kauravas, only three survived the end of this war of brothers.

This is the basic framework of the Mahabharata, the red thread so to speak. The heroes of the war—some themselves of divine origins—kept asking their heavenly protectors for new weapons, whenever one was threatened with defeat in a battle. And the gods heard their pleas, evidently without displaying much sensitivity. This meant that unbelievable weapons were being used, all from the arsenal of the Celestial Ones. The latter flew around in their vimanas or enjoyed the dolce vita in gigantic space cities—while human beings bled to death on the battlefields.

For example, the hero Vasudeva begged his god Agni (God of Fire) for a new weapon, and the latter made him a present of the disc *Charka*. This disc had a handle made of metal in the center and would always return to Vasudeva, even if the enemy had been vanquished. This is what happens in the second chapter of the Mahabharata. The disc strikes down warriors and even slices off the head of a well-protected king, then flies back to Vasudeva. Uncanny.

In the Pana Parva (the third Book of the Mahabharata), Arjuna asks his God Shiva for a weapon. Shiva gives it to him with the following words:

> *I will give you my favorite weapon, Pashupata. No one, not even the highest among the gods, knows it. You must be very careful, so that you do not use it incorrectly, because if you employ it against a weak enemy, you could destroy the whole world. There is nobody who cannot be destroyed with this weapon. You can fire it with a bow, or with your eye or even with the power of your intellect.*

Then Arjuna is instructed in the secrets of the use of this weapon. Shortly afterwards, the demi-god Kuvera joins them. He gives Arjuna the weapon called *Antardhana*. This weapon has the facility instantaneously to put all enemies to sleep. A hypnosis weapon? Finally, Indra, Lord of the Heavens, appears personally in a celestial battle chariot and invites Arjuna to climb into the flying vehicle and to visit the celestial realms with him. The Vana Parva (part of the Mahabharata) tells that Kaurava was also invited to visit the above-earthly realms:

> *You need to ascend to the heavens. Prepare yourself therefore. My own celestial vehicle, with Matali as the pilot [charioteer] will soon fly to Earth. He will take you into the celestial realms, and I promise to give you all my celestial weapons.*[12]

I have tried to translate, from English translations of the nineteenth century, those passages that are unavailable in German. In doubtful cases, where several options exist, I will provide the English original text. The following passage originates from division XLII of the Vana Parva that carries the title *Indralokagamana Parva* (part of the Mahabharata):

> *And while Gudakesha, equipped with great intelligence, was still considering, the vehicle, equipped with mighty superiority and driven by Matali, appeared from the clouds. It lit up the entire firmament and filled the area with great noise, like thunder. Missiles of terrible kind and . . . winged darts of celestial splendour and lights of shining splendour, as well as lightning bolts and "tutagudas" [untranslatable], equipped with wheels, and they worked on atmospheric expansion and created noise like the thunder from many clouds—all this was part of the flying vehicle. And the celestial vehicles had wild "nagas" [untranslatable, probably something serpent-like], with hot openings . . . And the celestial vehicle lifted off as if drawn by a thousand golden horses and quickly attained the speed of the wind. Very quickly, however, the celestial vehicle attained such a speed through its own integral power, that the eye could hardly mark its progress. And Arjuna saw a kind of "flag-staff," called*

"Vaijayanta" on the celestial vehicle, and of a shining gleam that resembles the colour of a dark emerald and was equipped with golden, shining ornaments . . . Arjuna said, "O Matali, Wonderful One, how you drive this celestial vehicle without losing time, as if hundreds of horses were united with the power. Even kings with all their great wealth . . . are not in a position to drive this celestial vehicle . . ." And Arjuna drove upwards with the magic object, the sun-like chariot, the celestial vehicle, he the wise offspring of Kuru's generation. The celestial vehicle moved with extraordinary speed and rapidly became invisible to the mortals on the Earth.

Division XLIII:

And the celestial city of Indra, where Arjuna arrived, was enchanting and also a place of recuperation for "siddhas" and "charanas". . . . And Arjuna saw the celestial gardens in which heavenly music could be heard. And then, up high, where the sun no longer shines, nor the moon, where fire no longer glows, but where everything shines with its own light, Arjuna saw other celestial vehicles, thousands of them, that were capable of movement anywhere at will, stationed in their proper places. Then he noticed ten thousand of these vehicles that were moving in all directions. What is seen as stars from Earth, looking like lamps because of the great distance, are in reality enormous bodies.[13]

In this fantastical story, which took place thousands of years ago somewhere in space, it is further reported that Arjuna visits all departments of this space habitat and is shown tests of the most diverse weapons of the Celestial Beings. He himself has to learn to control these terrible weapons. The training program, in the midst of the luxury of the celestial beings, lasts for a full five years. Arjuna is even instructed in the use of musical instruments that were only for the use of the celestial ones and "did not exist in the world of humans."

This all sounds like fairy tales, but it is not. Real things are being described here. I remember conversations in which it was said, again and again, that humans just have this desire for an ultimate weapon if they are hard pressed. Maybe. But not weapons that would have had no place in the world of Stone Age man, such as hypnosis weapons.

It has been objected that humans simply observed the birds, peacefully flying circles in the air, and humans just have this desire to copy the birds. Great. But birds do not make a hideous noise and do not cause hills and valleys to tremble. Birds do not need pilots who require special training on top of everything else. Birds also do not dispose of motors with some kind of mercury drive. And birds certainly do not fly into outer space.

Arjuna, the hero of the Mahabharata, was definitely there, and not in a land of dreams. Finally, there is a description of neither the Sun nor the Moon shining, but everything shining in its own light. We hear that thousands of other flying vehicles were parked up there, and because of the great distance from Earth, they looked like lamps but were, in reality, huge bodies.

No, my dear friends of the other faculty, we will get no further with psychology or humbug. People on Earth, staring at the sky, would be more likely to think that the Sun shines even more brightly up there than on the Earth. But the opposite is the case: it is dark in space. You do not dream that up. Whoever negates the description of space cities, space vehicles, shuttles, and thousands of flying vehicles in the Mahabharata just does not want it to be true because it does not fit into his or her concept of the world.

The notion that there never could have been a space vehicle in the dim and distant past actually contradicts the rules of evolution, according to which we humans have gone through a similar development. But if evolution turns out to be a continuous process, I would like an explanation for all the strange descriptions of celestial vehicles suddenly appearing all over the world in the old books. Why did our ancestors always report on gods who come from the heavens? Where did these, our ancestors, who had just said goodbye to the Stone Age, get the construction drawings for the described celestial vehicles? Where did they get knowledge about the alloys used and the navigation instruments? Even the "gods" would not have flown without instruments. These were not toy kites or hot air balloons. The vimanas disposed of several stories, were as large as temples, and had speeds that birds could only dream of.

There is not a single line in Sanskrit literature that refers to technicians, factories, or test flights. The celestial vehicles were suddenly there. Gods created them and flew them. Innovations, planning, and execution did not happen on our planet. There was no evolution of these things, nothing that could be developed step by step. If we had had such technology, humankind would have landed on Mars thousands of years ago! The flying vehicles described in the Indian texts were far ahead of our present technology. They could fly around the Earth, reach the Moon quite easily, stand still in space, when and where they wanted, and they had energies at their disposal that we cannot even imagine. More than sixty years ago, Loren Eiseley, professor of anthropology at the University of Pennsylvania and researcher of evolution, realized that something could not be right:

> *We have every reason to believe that, regardless of the forces that were involved in the formation of the human brain, a tough, long-drawn out battle for survival between several groups of human beings could not possibly have brought forth the high spiritual faculties that we observe among all peoples of the Earth today. Something else, a different formation factor, must have escaped the notice of evolution theoreticians.*[14]

Exactly so. Professor Eiseley is in good company today. More and more anthropologists and geneticists who study the laws of genetics on a molecular basis have noticed this too. The missing formation factor has a name: the gods. The annoying thing is that the new insights have barely been broadcast via the media because antiquated attitudes still rule the roost in these institutions.

If one accepts the factor of "gods" (extraterrestrials) in just one example, the antiquated texts from outside India suddenly become clear too. Right down to the quarrelsome and jealous God of the Old Testament. This simple insight also throws light on certain building technologies of prehistory. Once they are accepted, enlightenment will occur all over the world.

> *Steered by Matali, suddenly lighting up the sky, looking like tongues of fire without smoke, or like a glowing meteor in the clouds, the celestial vehicle appeared.*[15] *[Mahabharata, section CLXV, Nivata-Kavacha-yuddha Parva]*

Birds? Dreams? Hocus pocus?

Still invisible, the Daityas began to fight with the help of illusions. And I fought with them and used the energy of the invisible weapons . . . And when the Daityas fled and everything became visible again, hundreds of thousands of murdered people lay on the Earth . . . I became unsure, and Matali noticed this. When he saw how shocked I was, he said, "O Arjuna, Arjuna! Do not be afraid. Use the weapon of thunder and lightning." When I heard these words, I discharged that favourite weapon of the king of the celestials.[16] [Mahabharata, section CLXXII, Nivata-Kavacha-yuddha Parva]

Silly fantasies? Hardly, as when the weapon was used, it shattered entire mountains and valleys, burnt forests, and caused terrible destruction in the ranks of the enemies.

In the meantime, a different battle was taking place in the heavens. As the celestials had now evidently taken the part of one or the other of the sides of the earthlings, the gods too now began to shoot each other down. In the third chapter of the book Sabha-parvan (part of the Mahabharata), celestial cities of different sizes are described. They are led by Indra, Brahma, Rudra, Yama, Kuvera, and Varuna. These celestial cities were given the collective term *sabha*. They were of immense proportions and, seen from Earth, they shone like copper, gold, or silver. In these cities there were foods of all kinds, as well as water in great volumes, gardens and streams, living areas, and assembly halls. There were giant hangars for the vimanas and, of course, for the terrible weapons. One of these cities that revolved around itself was called Hiranyaoura (city of gold) and was originally built by Brahma. Two others were called

Gaganacara and Khecara. Over time, these cities became inhabited by evil beings, called *demons* in the Mahabharata. These demons had taken the side of the wrong party of humans. The top god Indra appears to have taken a dim view of this situation because he ordered the destruction of these celestial cities. Arjuna was given the task of carrying out this destruction, as he had spent five years being instructed in the use of the terrible weapons. He also had at his disposal the best pilot of a spaceship, Matali. Nor was Arjuna alone, as other spaceships with trained fighter pilots supported him.

A regular space battle took place. The demons knew how to keep on making their gigantic space structures invisible. They too disposed of treacherous weapons that they used to repulse the attacking adversaries for a while. The celestial cities of the demons were catapulted far out into space, and Arjuna waited for a good position to aim:

> When the three cities met in space, he shot through them with a terrible beam of three-fold fire. The daemons were incapable of countering this ray, which was ensouled with Yuga fire and was put together with Vishnu and Soma. While these three cities began to burn, Parvati rushed up to watch the spectacle.[17]

I mentioned this battle in space in my earlier books, but this time I had an even older translation at my disposal. All the translators from the nineteenth century translated the passages in the same way, although none of them at their time (between 1860 and 1890) could have had the foggiest idea of celestial cities. All of them used the phrases "celestial cities in the sky" and "the three cities came together in the firmament."

Today, mighty space cities in which battles are fought between rival races are nothing new in TV sci-fi series. All of this was already being described in ancient Indian literature. It just does not fit if we follow the usual simplistic evolutionary thought patterns. Logically, this is obvious. The same goes for the weapons of the gods, which are used in the Mahabharata, for example:

This weapon caused fear and dismay when Kama got it out of the armaments store . . . The birds in the air put up a terrible racket, a violent storm arose, lightning flashed and thunder rolled. The weapon plunged with a great noise into the heart of Ghatotka-chas, bored through it and disappeared in the starry night sky.

Aswathama flung his most dangerous weapon "Narayana" against the Pandava troops. It flew up in the air, thousands of darts came down like hissing serpents and fell on all sides onto the warriors. Vasudeva begged the troops to cease fighting and to throw away their weapons because he knew that the Narayana weapon would proceed according to a magic charm. It would kill all those who fought or wanted to fight, while it would leave unharmed those who had thrown away their weapons.[18]

One of the brave ones, Bhima, did not want to throw away his weapon, and he quickly became enveloped in a sea of flames. Then Arjuna stepped onto the battlefield and used the divine weapon *Baruna*. It quenched the fire, but this happened only after Bhima finally threw away his weapon.

We are familiar with multiple-rocket launchers today, but we do not know of missiles that will attack only enemies who are carrying weapons. How does that work? Much is possible with the gods, and in the Mahabharata, even nuclear weapons are employed:

> *Following his command, Arjuna fired the weapons that had the power of repulsing destruction . . . The weapons flew high in the air and flames broke out of them that resemble the great fire that consumes the earth at the end of a world epoch. Thousands of shooting stars fell from the sky, the animals in the waters and on land trembled with fear. The Earth shook . . . At that moment, the most famous sage living at the time approached, Veda Vyasa . . . he urgently advised [someone] to withdraw the weapon, which he had unleashed. If he did not do so, Arjuna would counter this weapon with his "Brahmastra" which was infallible. If things went that far, however, twelve years of drought would befall the land. Arjuna knew this and therefore, had for the well being of humankind, always held back, so as to save them. Aswathama should, therefore, immediately withdraw his weapon and give up his precious stone . . . Aswathama spoke, ". . . This infallible weapon will even kill all unborn children . . ." This is why all the children that were born, were dead.*

This is not the only passage in the Mahabharata that refers to lethal radiation. The following quote originates from the fifth book of the Mahabharata and was translated as early as 1891:

> *The sun appeared to turn in a circle. Singed by the heat of the weapons, the Earth swayed in the heat. Elephants were burnt and ran wildly about, back and forth . . .*
> *The raging fire caused trees to fall in great swathes, as in a forest fire . . . horses and chariots burned, everything looked like it does after a terrible conflagration. Thousands of vehicles were destroyed, then a deep stillness came over the Earth . . . a*

dreadful sight was seen. The corpses of the slain had been muti-
lated by the terrible heat; they no longer looked like humans. We
have never before seen such a terrible weapon and have never
before heard of such a weapon . . . It is like a brilliant lightning,
a frightful herald of death, which has caused all the followers of
the Vrishni and the Andhaka to crumble to ash. The burnt out
bodies were unrecognisable. The survivors found that their hair
and nails fell out. Pottery goods would break without cause, the
surviving birds turned white. Within a short time, food became
toxic. The lightning sank down and turned to fine dust.[19]

Additional information is given in the eighth book of
the Mahabharata, the Musala Parva. There you can read that
Curkha, one of the gods, shot a single missile on the three-fold
city, brighter than the Sun. The elephants roared and burned,
all the birds fell from the sky, food became toxic; the warriors
who were not directly involved threw themselves into streams
and lakes, "as all had been covered in the lethal breath of the
god. The unborn children died in their mothers' wombs."

No, dear skeptics, we have to own up here. What the
chroniclers of thousands of years ago described did not originate out of any macabre fantasies. A former reality has been
recorded here. Nobody could know anything about such
dreadful weapons before Hiroshima and Nagasaki in the
Second World War. Nobody could know that radioactivity
makes any kind of food toxic; nobody could know that radioactivity in connection with a divine lightning strike, brighter
than the Sun, could kill unborn children in their mothers'
wombs. Nobody could know that remnant radioactivity could
make *hair and nails fall out.* Why? *Everything had been covered*
with the deadly breath of the god.

Traces of these weapons of the gods can still be found in the Sumerian-Babylonian epic of Gilgamesh, fifth tablet:

The Heavens screamed, the earth roared a response, a flash of lightning, a fire flared up, death rained down. The brightness disappeared, the fire died down. Everything that had been hit by the lightning turned to ash.

And in the eighth tablet, Gilgamesh asks his dying friend Enkidu, "Did the toxic breath of the celestial animal hit you?"[20]

Why should our ancestors' imagination come up with something as absurd as a bird causing a "toxic breath" that had a lethal effect? Why was Aswathama in the Mahabharata supposed to give up his "precious stone" and thereby withdraw a terrible weapon? What was meant by that precious stone? Some kind of command vehicle that had been built in the weapons factories of the gods? These gods were hypocrites; from a human point of view, they could actually be labeled criminals. They equipped their favorites with dreadful weapons of destruction and watched them exterminate each other. The humans appeared to play the parts of extras in all this. Human life appeared to have no value for the gods. The gods had, after all, created humans; the gods ruled over life and death, like we do over the life and death of ants. Time evidently played a minor role for these gods. They knew that humans would multiply again—like ants. I have little sympathy for that type of god.

Nobody who has studied the ancient Indian literature can doubt that these gods used the most varied kinds of space-worthy flying vehicles. Sanskrit expert Professor Kanjilal has pointed to forty-one text passages alone in the Vana Parva (part of the Mahabharata).[21] Here are the most important passages:

O you, Uparicara Vasu, the roomy flying machine will come to you. (Ch. 63, 11–16)

O you, offspring of the Kurus, that evil person came with the self-propelled flying vehicle that can move anywhere and is known as Saubhapura. (Ch. 42, 15–22)

When he had disappeared from the sight of the mortals, high up in the sky, he noticed thousands of strange flying vehicles. (Ch. 42, 30–34)

He stepped into Indra's divine favorite palace and saw thousands of flying vehicles for the gods, some that had been parked, some that were in motion. (Ch. 43, 7–12)

The groups from Maruts came in celestial flying vehicles, and Matali took me with him in his flying vehicle and showed me the other flying vehicles. (Ch. 168, 10–11)

The gods appeared in their own flying vehicles in order to watch the battle between Kripacarya and Arjuna. Even Indra, the Lord of the Heavens, appeared with his special flying object, and with him were 33 celestial beings. (Ch. 274 ff and 275 ff)

He gave him a self-propelled flying vehicle, known as Puspaka. (Ch. 207, 6–9)

In the Kathasaritsagara, an Indian text collection from ancient times, a flying vehicle is mentioned that "never has to be refuelled" and transports people to far-away countries beyond the sea. There, the astonished reader is told of a flying vehicle that was able to cover—non-stop—a distance of 3,200 kilometers, calculated in our own terms, as well as another flying vehicle of King Narabahanadutta, in which 1,000 men were transported on a single flight to Kausambi (Ch. 43, 21 ff).

In the fifth century AD, the greatest dramatic artist and poet of India, Kalidasa, lived at the court of the Indian Gupta-kings. He adapted material from the Mahabharata and Ramayana in his epics and dramas, as he also did in the work called *Raghuwamsha*. The various stages of the flight of Rama to Ajodhja are described in clear detail and with astonishing scientific exactitude. One reads about the phenomenal view of the heaving oceans and the mountains under water. The flying vehicle of Rama was able to attain different altitudes— sometimes it flew about in the clouds, then below the birds, and sometimes along the paths "frequented by the gods [in their vehicles]" (Ch. 13, 19). The flying vehicle flew over the entire Highland of Decan, including the Alyaban Mountains, then a lake and the Godavari River, the hermitage of Agastya, as well as that of Sasabhanga, and finally the mountain called Chitrakuta. Then it went on, above the confluence of the rivers Ganges and Jammuna, past the capital city of the King of Nisada, in the direction of Uttarakosala on the Saraju River. When the vehicle landed in Uttarakosala, a crowd of people gathered. Rama, followed by his passengers, left the vehicle via a glittering stair made of metal (Ch. 13, 69). After meeting the ruler of the place, Rama and his company boarded his flying machine again via the same metal stair. The flight route, which can easily be reconstructed today, comprised about 2,500 kilometers.

The same dramatist Kalidasa also reported a journey by air in Indra's celestial vehicle that was, once again, piloted by Matali. The flying device moved through moist clouds, where the wheels were retracted. It climbed up to higher altitudes where there was no more air for breathing, but also flew so low over the dense forest foliage that the birds fled in fright. After landing, Duhsantra remarked that one of the passengers was surprised that the wheels had not whirled up dust and did not even touch the ground. The pilot Matali kindly explained that this hovering above the ground was thanks to the superior technology of Indra. Did Indra possess an anti-gravitation device?

Kalidasa was a poet who compiled comedies in addition to his dramas. Fantasy was his forte; it belongs to the repertoire of the poet. But even fantasy needs stimulation. Kalidasa found this in the much older epics of the Mahabharata and the Ramayana. So, what is this Ramayana?

The word *Ramayana* means "Rama's Life." The origins of the events are lost somewhere in ancient India. The Ramayana reports on a king of the Sun dynasty, who once inhabited Ajodhja. The king had four sons by four different women, with Rama, the eldest, far outstripping his brothers in all fields. This was why his father chose him as his successor. A maternal intrigue prevented this succession, and Rama had to leave the country for fourteen years. Rama had a beautiful wife, called Sita, who was kidnapped by Rawana, the ruler of Lanka (Ceylon, now Sri Lanka). (The same kind of event provided the impulse for the Trojan War in Greece.) Clever Rama built a bridge to connect India with Lanka, and it was later used by his troops. Rama himself fetched his beloved Sita back with the help of his flying vimanas. At last, Rama was able to sit on the throne of his father. A happy end.

The framework of the story is simple, but the technology used is rather dramatic. Two types of flying vehicles are employed in the Ramayana: the vimanas and the rathas. The first moved extremely fast, were pointed at the front, and contained several luxurious chambers. They even had pearl-encrusted windows, and all the inside chambers were laid with carpets. Most vimanas mentioned in the Ramayana could transport twelve passengers. A flight between Lanka and Vasisthasrama is described in some detail. Today this would correspond to a distance of about 2,880 kilometers, which could be traveled within a few hours. In contrast to the Mahabharata, in the Ramayana it is predominantly humans who pilot these extraordinary flying vehicles, usually trained leaders of armies or kings. Trained, naturally, by the gods. It should be emphasized again that the technology for the construction of the vimanas came from the gods. Humans did not invent anything. Clear distinctions are made between humans who are allowed to fly a vimana and the gods in their phenomenal celestial cities.

What did these gods actually want here originally? They are supposed to have come to Earth in very early times to study humans. What a wonderful study, considering the devastating wars they instigated! In fact, the gods are supposed to have been here in even earlier times to create humans, which did not seem to have been a great success; otherwise, they would not have had to kill them again subsequently.

For those skeptical students of India but also for interested laypersons who would like to check all this, a few flight scenes from the Ramayana follow:

Together with Khara he climbed into the flying vehicle that was adorned with jewels. It made a great noise that resembled thunder from the clouds. (Ch. 3, 35, 6–7)

You may go where you wish, I will take Sita to Lanka by air . . . so Rama and Maricha climbed into the flying vehicle that resembled a palace. (Ch. 3, 42, 7–9)

Do you scoundrel believe you can attain wealth by getting yourself this flying vehicle? (Ch. 3, 30, 12)

The flying vehicle, which had the speed of thought, appeared again in Lanka. (Ch. 4, 48, 25–37)

This is the excellent flying vehicle called Puspaka and it shines like the sun. (Ch. 4, 123, 1)

The flying object . . . rose in the air with a loud noise. (Ch. 4, 123, 1)

All the harem ladies of the monkey king quickly finished decorating and climbed into the celestial vehicle. (Ch. 4, 123, 1–55)

I have already given an outline of the framework of the story. In the discussion about Rama and Sita, I told how the scoundrel Rawana abducted the enchanting Sita in a "vehicle of the air that resembled the sun." The flight took them across high hills and forests. Neither the kidnapped Sita's cries for help nor her pleas could persuade her abductor to turn back. When Rama heard about the abduction, he gave a curt military command, "Get out the vehicle of the air!"

In the meantime, Rawana, the evil one, was already flying above the ocean in the direction of Lanka. But Rama's flying vehicle was faster. He caught up with Rawana and challenged him to an aerial battle. He shot down the abduction vehicle with a "celestial dart," and it plunged into the ocean. Sita was rescued and climbed into the celestial vehicle belonging to her husband, who climbed high up into a cumulus cloud with a mighty racket.

Rama, the hero of the Ramayana, had clever allies. One of these gifted comrades was the king of the monkeys called Hanuman. The king of the monkeys was able to transform himself into a giant or a dwarf at will. He was also a daredevil pilot. When he began his flight from the mountains, the tops of the rocks broke off, giant trees were toppled, and the mountains vibrated. Birds and animals fled in terror to their deepest retreats. Sometimes this daredevil pilot would start off from a city. Then the ponds and lakes would overflow, and the vimana would "lift off with its burning tail above the roofs and start great fires, so that the buildings and all the towers would collapse and the pleasure gardens were devastated."

Truly, a terrible flying vehicle. But then it did originate from the workshops of the gods, and they really did not care a fig about the destroyed houses of human beings. Whenever I read in the Indian texts that flying vehicles had started great fires, ruined gardens, and toppled towers, I always think of the Kebra Negest, the book of the Ethiopian Kings.[22] In this book, Baina-lehkem, a son of King Solomon, had flown across Egypt, en route from Jerusalem to Ethiopia. The Egyptians complained that the flying vehicle had caused statues of the gods and obelisks to fall down ("because they drove a vehicle like the angels, and they were faster than the eagles in the sky").

The holy (less today) writings of India, the Vedas, contain descriptions that can only be understood in our times. I recognize a certain logic in this. Naturally, the celestials, those vain-glorious gods, knew that humans at that time were unable to understand their technology. The same can be seen today in the ethnologically accepted notion of the "cargo-cult."[23] For human beings in those days, this celestial technology seemed like something from the realm of magic. Celestial stuff. But educated people were *meant* to report on this. There was method behind it all. Only thanks to the traditions from those legendary times were people of the future—we!—able to know what was happening in those days. And it was precisely this knowledge that would provoke us future ones to pose new questions that would never have been *without* the old texts. When in 1968, in my first book *Chariots of the Gods?*, I came up with the provocative question as to whether our ancestors might have had visitors from space thousands of years ago, I had not snatched the question out of thin air. Certain indicators forced me to ask the question. But only after posing the question about whether our ancestors had visitors from space did new types of questions become possible. Extraterrestrials? Do they even exist? What do they look like? Why should they have visited us? Why us? Why at that time, of all times? What technology did they use? How did they overcome the distances of light years? How did they even know that we existed? Why did they do what they did? What was their motivation? Have they left any evidence behind? Might they be coming back? If so, when? How would we respond? And so on, and so on. This entire catalogue of questions is only possible *after* posing the question about whether our ancestors might have had visitors from space. *Before* that, the main question had never been posed—and so there were no other questions. This is precisely the method I see behind it all. A kind of paperchase, so that people in the future should be forced to ask the right questions and finally arrive at the right answers.

In all this, it does not matter whether the people in those days understood what they were seeing and experiencing, nor in what mystical, nebulous manner they recorded their experiences. The content alone, no matter what the packaging, should make people in the future pause with suspicion. And that is exactly what they are doing. You have succeeded, you up there! In the Rigveda, for example, technologies, but also philosophical thoughts, are described that do not fit into any category in those days. Here are a few tasters:

> *All who leave this Earth will first all go to the Moon . . . the Moon is the gateway to outer space, and whoever is able to answer his questions is allowed to proceed beyond it. (Rig Veda, 1, Adhyana)*[24]

Naturally, the Moon is the exit base for interplanetary and interstellar journeys. Spaceships of great size are able to take off from the Moon because of its low gravitational force. Or the ships can be assembled from a kit in orbit around the Moon, which is much easier there than in an orbit around the Earth. Certainly, these components had to be shipped first from the Earth to the Moon, but takeoffs to the mother ship that is being built are much easier from the surface of the Moon or from an orbit around the Moon than from Earth. The thing is, no human being living thousands of years ago could have known this.

> *Space is far greater than the Fire [the Sun], as space contains*
> *both Sun and Moon, lightning, stars and fire. By virtue of space*
> *one calls out, one hears, one answers; in space you are happy*
> *and are not; one is born in space, one is born for space; may you*
> *worship space. Whosoever worships space, he will attain space*
> *wealth, worlds rich in light, unrestricted, for striding far and*
> *wide, and as far as space extends, he shall be able to roam there*
> *at will. (Rig Veda)*[25]

All of these statements are true. Now we just need to filter out the original meaning. Sentences like "Whosoever worships space, he will attain space wealth" could be translated as "Whosoever *undertakes* space research, he will attain space wealth." India expert Professor Kanjilal in Calcutta told me that the Sanskrit word stem of "to worship" and "to undertake" was the same, as human beings undertake worship. Being *born in space and for space* is an old idea for any astronaut. In future, spaceships will be built for entire generations of people; they will live, love, die, and be born on board. The thing is: nobody could have known this thousands of years ago.

When I read in the Mahabharata that Indra, the highest of those gods, explains to Arjuna, that *Time is the seed of the universe,* then bells start ringing for me, perhaps not for others. Ask a modern astrophysicist when or how Time began? Time began at the same time as the universe began. Time *is* the seed of the universe. When I read that Arjuna had been instructed in the use of musical instruments in the celestial city and that these instruments were restricted to use by the celestials and did not exist in the world of humans, I could turn cartwheels with joy. Why? Because here (as elsewhere) clear distinctions are made between the celestials and us humans. They were not all the same.

When I read a passage like, *steered by Matali, suddenly lighting up the sky, looking like tongues of fire without smoke, or like a glowing meteor in the clouds,* roses start blooming for me. Why? In various passages, Matali is explicitly made to stand out as the pilot of Indra's celestial vehicles. The people staring upward recognize the tongues of flame around the vehicle but are surprised that this fire is not accompanied by *any smoke* and, moreover, compare the thing with a meteor. A meteor is an object in the sky, which has a tail behind it (to human eyes). Indra's flying ship was compared with a *glowing meteor,* which spews *tongues of fire without smoke.* What more could one want?

If I read about a terrible weapon *that humankind has never experienced before,* a weapon that *makes all food toxic and also kills unborn children in their mothers' wombs,* then I know, as a world citizen in the twenty-first century, what is meant. But the people thousands of years ago could not know. Any more questions?

We today are bewildered, and this bewilderment is the result of thousands of years of indoctrination by religions. Every Earthling has been brainwashed with having to feel enveloped by God everywhere, and that he can be watched by God, even in the most secret place. This requires a God-Spirit who has to be omnipresent. Only a God-Spirit can do everything and penetrate everything. The universe is God—pantheism, the teaching that everything is God, dominates in all religious-philosophical teachings in which God and the world are identical. God has to be an impersonal being in the sense of these teachings. The great philosopher Arthur Schopenhauer (1788–1860) referred to this interpretation as "polite atheism." Even in Christianity, which allows the son of God to appear as a human being, there is a portion of pantheism; otherwise, the Christian God could not be omnipresent. God has to be Spirit. Omnipresent, almighty, and omniscient, he possesses the omnipotent gift to know in advance what is ever going to happen. Standing above everything in this way, human concerns are foreign to "him." As a God-Spirit he would not require an objective, visible vehicle to move from one place to another. Spirit is everywhere. Exactly: IT.

Whether it is the Old Testament or ancient Indian religion, *the* God or the gods who manifested there used vehicles, were not infallible, used terrible weapons, destroyed innocent children, and favored certain parties. Where is the logic in this? Whoever it was playing with human beings in those days, it was not God.

Old Indian texts list metal alloys and liquids that were used as fuels, quicksilver or mercury among them. What is mercury, actually? Mercury has the characteristics of a precious metal; it is very constant in a pure state. At a temperature of $-38.83°C$, the silvery substance solidifies into a crystalizing mass that is lighter than lead. It will begin to boil at $357°C$. It does, however, evaporate slowly even at low temperatures; mercury vapor is released, which is very toxic. This strange metal will dissolve most other metals, like gold, silver, copper, lead, and even platinum—although at higher temperatures. Curiously, it does not do the same to iron, nickel, silicon, or manganese. How can mercury be contained if it dissolves even gold? It will only work with glass, iron, or glazed ceramics (jars). Where is it derived from? It is easily obtained from ores, as even steam from water or vinegar is sufficient to dissolve out the mercury. In classical times, the element mercury was assigned to the planet Mercury. Many peoples worked it. (Aristotle of Greece, 384 BC, referred to it as "liquid silver" and Theophrastus, 315 BC, described the extraction of the metal.) Mercury and mercury vapor form the most varied compounds, which are used in all manner of industrial processes and for other uses.

If we follow the statements made in the ancient Indian texts, mercury was used as a fuel, which was transported in the vimana, either in a container made of iron, in a jug, or in a container made of mica. I am always amazed by facts that archaeologists pile into somewhere and which they are incapable of assigning to any category. Mercury was found in the tomb of the Chinese Quin dynasty Emperor Shihuangdi, whose dates are disputed. Large quantities of mercury! In March 1974, farmers drilling for water near Lingtong (Shaanxi Province) came upon a burial mound, in which about 7,000 clay imperial soldiers were later found. They were all lined up ready to march. (In passing, the 7,000 figures alone pointed to an industrial-style production.) Gradually, models of several rivers were discovered, sealed watertight with layers of clay—the Yangtze, the Huanghe, and the sea, all made of mercury. Above them had been modeled a splendid firmament with many celestial bodies. Large quantities of mercury in the tomb of a mystical emperor from China—is this a unique find? But no, 25,000 kilometers away by air, there was another amazing discovery of mercury.

Copan, in present-day Honduras, is considered to be the "Paris of the Maya world." Copan appears gigantic with its pyramids and temples. The meanings of many puzzling sculptures and so-called anthropomorphic depictions have not been clarified to this day. The city of Copan once controlled an important jade deposit in the Motagua Valley. Jade was more important than gold for the Maya. The "hieroglyph stairway" from Copan is well known, and has the king list of Copan chiseled into its fifty-six steps. This work was carried out by a king called Butz'Yip, which means something like "smoke is his strength." What smoke?

Anthropomorphic sculptures from Copan (Honduras),
the meaning of which remains a mystery to this day.

Gods or human figures? Nobody knows. This Copan figure
appears to be tapping a keyboard on its chest.

Ricardo Agurcia, director of the excavations on the Copan
project, discovered a subterranean temple there in 1992. The
part above ground is called Temple 16; the subterranean
one, Rosalia. Naturally, Rosalia is much older than Temple
16 because the latter was built over Rosalia. "You come out of
this low tunnel—and suddenly you stand in front of a huge
wall, 12 m tall, the façade of the old temple, brilliant blue, red
and ochre," wrote the excavator Nikolai Grube. Masks with
gods' or human faces hung on the colorful wall, as well as the
"more than 2–m-tall mask of the top bird god with numerous,
well-preserved ornaments."[26] From here a shaft leads down
even further; on the steps are several Maya glyphs that even the
best specialists (Linda Schele and Nikolai Grube) were unable
to decipher. Not until later, with the help of a computer, did
the decipherers come to believe that the temple had been
consecrated by a king called Moon-Jaguar. Finally, the experts

managed to uncover the foundations of Rosalia, and there they believed they had hit the tomb of the dynasty's founder, Yax K'uk'Mo.

Indefinable spherical shapes appear in both the anthropomorphic sculptures and in the figures at Copan. Symbolic energy?

However, no excavator was able to enter the tomb, as it was filled to the brim with highly toxic mercury! Do we get an inkling of something here?

In the meantime, an expert in a protective suit climbed into the mercury-filled vault and discovered that it was not the founder of the dynasty lying in the tomb, but a woman. A little deeper down was a further chamber. A male burial "with high quality grave goods" is supposed to have been viewed through a shaft.[27] There seems to be silence on the subject of what high-quality burial goods these might have been—as always whenever things are inexplicable or even mysterious.

By the way, tourists may admire a perfect copy of Rosalia, with its fearful masks, in the new Museum of Copan. While looking at these, one is almost transported back to ancient India, but this is often the case in Central America. One need only compare the ornamentation or the gestures made by the statues, both here and there, or compare the temple pyramids in Central America with those in India. What did it say in the Kathasaritsagara, that collection of Indian texts from ancient times? "The flying vehicle never had to take up fuel and took people to far countries across the seas."

Our archaeologists lack imagination—because they are not allowed to have any. Archaeology is a dyed-in-the-wool conservative branch of research, carried out by witty, humorous scientists, for the most part with great integrity. Inevitably, at their universities, they are required to swat up on the homogenous mix of teaching that stubbornly orientates itself on the evolutionary principle. Everything has developed slowly, constantly, one thing after the other. The specialist for Central America knows nothing about Indian myths; he is not interested in them. The specialist for Egypt has not the foggiest notion of the phenomenal prehistoric buildings in the highlands of Peru. The India expert has never studied the Old Testament, knows nothing about technical descriptions of a spaceship in the book of the prophet Ezekiel. If he or she did know, presumably he or she would make those cross-connections. But just a moment! This cannot be, because it is one of the dogmas of classical research that there were no connections between one continent and the other thousands of years ago.

Extraterrestrials? Real gods thousands of years ago? Impossible! Put on your hairshirt and repent! And any expert who still has a modicum of ability to make free associations will not dare to discuss with colleagues the finds that do not fit into the picture, let alone write about them. He would immediately become subject to ridicule. That which is not allowed to be cannot be. So one should not be surprised if highly interesting finds are swept under the carpet and are never made public. Even worse: Not even the other experts in the field are given a chance to hear about these mysterious finds.

The same system applies to our media. A journalist who wishes to advance, to become an arts editor or even chief editor, first has to have proved that he or she has the specialist knowledge and the proper—serious—outlook. Both originate in that old homogenous mix. Just as an archaeologist may not publicly report on a sensational find that does not fit into any framework, a journalist who wishes to be taken seriously cannot write a really sensational piece of news without having first covered his or her own back with the experts. But the latter do not do this. With this really well-functioning system, we need not wonder any more whether society is stuck in yesterday's knowledge and is even brainwashed with the notion that the present knowledge is the pinnacle of all knowledge.

I am one of those people who, now and again, finds out something unusual from an expert. Naturally, this information is always proffered under an oath of secrecy, and fairness compels me to stick to the secrecy agreed on. The same goes for me. I would not wish to break a confidence and thereby subject that person to the knives of their colleagues. Moreover, I would destroy that human relationship, and the source of information would dry up. What can be done with this vicious circle? I help myself by asking the person who has told me something in confidence whether I would be allowed to pass on this or that piece of information. Sometimes they give me permission, but I am always begged not to give names. So, I stick to this agreement with both a good and an uncomfortable feeling. The good feeling is brought about by the fact that I have not got my informant into trouble, not exposed that person. The bad feeling is caused by the fact that I have kept back valuable information. Which has the priority? With me, it is my word. In the media world, this behavior is legally protected. No journalist can be forced to name his or her informants.

Added to this double bind—which assails everyone who does what I do—is the problem of one's own credibility. I am used to listing the sources of my information precisely so that they can be checked. I do not wish to appeal to faith, because faith is the domain of religion. Next, therefore, I will relate information without revealing my sources, and the reader will be resigned to either believing me or not.

The oldest tomb containing mercury was found in Copan. I know that similar discoveries have been made elsewhere in Maya country, in Tikal and Palenque. Mercury, according to the ancient Indians, served as a fuel, and mercury vapors, as we know today, are highly toxic. Why do so many of the top Maya priests wear masks? In India, there were even masks with hoses, similar to our gas masks. As we heard from the old Indian texts, mercury was transported in containers made of mica, among other materials. Why have subterranean mica chambers been found in Central America, not only among the Maya, but also among the Teotihuacanos in the highland of Mexico? Even if no mercury was discovered in these chambers—and I have to say I cannot be sure that the excavators were not fibbing a bit— this means very little. If a mica chamber is not properly sealed, the mercury may well have evaporated in the course of thousands of years. This, by the way, would explain the strange cases of deaths of high priests (the knowledgeable ones) and rulers.

The mica chamber in Teotihuacan, Mexico,
which was kept secret for a long time.

What exactly is mica? Mica is a substance that is created over millions of years in mountains. It is a compound of silicon, aluminum, and oxygen. Mica can be picked apart like the leaves of a book and can appear in various colors. Thin layers of mica have been used, even in the past, as windows in industrial furnaces because it is heat resistant. Mica can also be found in the electrical industry and in the building of antennae, as mica has proved to be an extremely good electrical insulator. This substance is even impervious to acids, at least to all organic acids.

Mica has been found in the ancient tombs of North American noblemen, often pejoratively referred to as chieftains. Did they know anything about the multiple functions of mica? And where does it come from? In 1983, a subterranean mica chamber was discovered in Teotihuacan, the giant complex at the edge of Mexico City (as I reported in my book *The Day the Gods Came*). For the first few years after the discovery, the authorities for archaeology and anthropology in Mexico City made a holy secret of it. Why? Moreover, no one can dispute that, after my publication in 1984, the secret crumbled away, and now for years tourists, if they insist, are allowed to admire the ceiling of the mica chamber. A warden will lift the metal cover, which was fitted after the discovery and is secured with padlocks. Could any archaeologist give me one convincing reason for this theater of secrecy? Normally, in these cases, talk is of "protecting" the artifact. Something has to be protected from the "stupid public." Sorry, but mica does not rust, is indestructible, and both lightning strikes and acids—which can arise from dead plants—are not able to affect it.

Now, the gullible tourist may believe that because the secret is no longer a secret, the authorities would have laid their cards on the table. I have to disappoint you. A tunnel leads into the Sun Pyramid of Teotihuacan—forbidden to tourists. In the center, underneath the pyramid, there are chambers—forbidden to tourists and researchers. There has never been a public announcement about what has been discovered in these chambers. And I would like to see *all* the objects, not just a few items that are agreeable and acceptable. There is something else the public has not been told—and I have this from a reliable source: a pipe insulated with mica runs out of one of these subterranean chambers. It would be revealing to trace the line of this pipe and find out where the pipe runs to and what is at the end of it. I have not yet heard about whether this has not been done already, secretly.

In the spring of 2001, American archaeologists discovered two tombs with prehistoric skeletons on a mound called Nabta—1,350 kilometers south of Cairo. Both tombs were not only decorated with paintings of the heavenly goddess Hathor but were also massively insulated with mica. Because no mica occurs naturally in this region, it must have been imported from the Sudanese mountains. Why and by whom, 4,000 years BC?

All this secretiveness stinks to high heaven, and what really drives me up the wall is the hypocritical fuss by the responsible authorities who always act as though there is no secretiveness at all. But it is definitely going on—and how! In 1993, German engineer Rudolf Gantenbrink conducted

research inside the pyramid of Cheops on a 20-by-20 centi-
meter shaft that is 62 meters long. At the end of the shaft, he
discovered a small door with two copper fittings or hinges. I
have previously reported on this.[28] There is no lack of funds
or technology to open this little door before the eyes of the
world. But what happens? Secretiveness. The Department of
Antiquities in Cairo has prevented an opening of the door
with unspeakably threadbare arguments. And if the opening
is to take place in secret or has perhaps already taken place,
the archaeologists responsible for the Great Pyramid have
lost every claim to credibility. They sit in their ivory towers
and still maintain indignantly that the public really ought to
believe their statements. They cannot understand that the
public has become critical and skeptical—as if there had not
been enough political and scientific misinformation during
the past few decades.

And while I am lifting the lid on these matters, here are a
few more remarks on present misinformation. After the publication of my book *Chariots of the Gods?*, a new organization
was set up in the USA, with the goal of exposing once and for
all this "nonsense" à la Däniken and Uri Geller and factually
informing the public about the truth. The Committee for Scientific Investigation of Claims of the Paranormal, or CSICOP
(now called the Committee for Skeptical Inquiry, or CSI), is the
name of the association in America (in Germany, it is called the
"Skeptiker" Organisation). Now every skeptic and critic is, of
course, free to state an opposing opinion vociferously and, if
they so wish, to be indignant. But please do not do this under
the pretense of delivering facts. Unfortunately, however, this

is what has been happening in the name of CSICOP. Robert Anton Wilson, the author of an informative book on CSICOP, remarks in his foreword:

> By the New Inquisition I mean to designate certain habits of repression and intimidation that are becoming increasingly commonplace in the scientific community today.[29]

So how does this work? You gather around you a few scientists who are naturally convinced that they are in no need of educating and know exactly what is possible and not possible. Using these reputable names, you then publish a magazine—in the case of CSICOP, it is *The Skeptical Inquirer.* The next step consists of getting TV-program makers, who rely on the good names of the scientists, to put together a TV series. In the English-speaking world, this is *Horizon,* produced by the BBC. Because both the BBC and the scientists who speak on the programs have a good reputation, the *Horizon* programs are soon broadcast all over the world. So? What is wrong with that? By editing and leaving out things, using interviews out of context, making misrepresentations or insinuations, and using targeted manipulation, the programs give the viewer an objective and seemingly true picture—while the reality of the matter is quite different. This last happened in October and November 1999.[30] Two researchers, Robert Bauval and Adrian Gilbert, had published a book entitled *The Orion Mystery* [in 1994] and had even reported on it in a TV documentary.[31] The two authors were able to demonstrate, with the help of Egyptologists and astronomers, that the Great Pyramids of Giza were aligned on the constellation of Orion and must, therefore, be much older than accepted archaeological wisdom believes.

The *Horizon* programs by the BBC tore up this opinion, misrepresented the statements by Robert Bauval, twisted the Orion picture, and did not even allow the astronomer who had worked on the decisive calculations for the new theory to speak. All in the name of scientific truth! An amazing explanation. Presumably, some of the good scientists who worked with CSICOP did not even know who pulls the strings behind this organization.

Today, every high school pupil knows what a DNA test is and that such a test can be used to convict criminals and confirm blood relationships. Some Japanese experts wanted to conduct DNA tests on Egyptian mummies to clarify, among other things, whether Tutankhamun's father was of royal blood. The Supreme Council of Antiquities in Cairo banned the project in the short term. Dr. Zahi Hawass, head of the Council of Antiquities, quickly explained to the news agency Associated Press why this had happened: "The results of these examinations could be used to re-write Egyptian history" and "There are people who would like to change Egyptian history."[32] And there are evidently also people who would like to prevent this.

There is no question of credibility where the ancient Indian texts are concerned. Nobody is required to *believe* in these texts, as their contents speak for themselves. And they are not concerned with beliefs. The statements alone, even if they are in a mythological package, are sufficient. The people of ancient India just cannot have known anything about the terrible weapons systems that were used and even less about vimanas of different kinds, let alone of habitats in space. But these things are still to be found in those texts, whether we like it or not.

Since the 1950s, a few Indian scholars—some of them sages or masters (swamis)—have been looking at these ancient Indian writings with modern eyes. Texts exist that have a religious veneer—for example, those of the Krishna movement. This does not change anything about the contents, as the age of the text is recorded. The following story is derived from the tenth hymn of the Srimad-Bhagavatam.[33]

This story tells of the battle between the Yalu dynasty and a demon called Salva, who had managed to obtain possession of a marvelous celestial vehicle with the name of Saubha. Salva turned to the demi-god Shiva to obtain additional forces to use against Krishna, whom he hated and wished to kill. Salva, therefore, asked Shiva for a flying city, which should be so powerful that it could not be destroyed by any demi-god, demon, human, Gandharva, or Naga, not even by a Raksasa. He also wanted this aerial city to be capable of flying anywhere. Shiva, the demi-god, agreed, and with the help of the phenomenal designer Maya—who is also mentioned with the same functions in the epics and the puranas—a truly frightening but stable flying complex was constructed that could not be destroyed by anybody. It was as large as a city and was able to fly so high and fast that it was practically impossible to see it. After Salva had taken over this marvelous flying vehicle, he flew off to attack the city of the Yadus, against whom he nursed an undying hatred.

Before attacking the city called Dwarka from the air, he had it surrounded by an immense army of foot soldiers. Both the strategically important parts of the city, but also all the parts in which the inhabitants congregated, came under attack. There was a reason for this. Salva could have destroyed the city from the air, but he wanted to get hold of a few selected people first. In addition, underneath the city lay defense forces against aerial attacks, which he needed to shut down first. Once the ground troops had been successful, Salva bombarded the city with lightning strikes, rocks, poisonous serpents, and other dangerous objects. He also managed to create a hurricane, which was so violent that it shrouded all of Dwarka in darkness by darkening the sky with dust.

Then the great heroes of Dwarka assembled and decided on a counter attack. Their leader was called Pradyumna, and he too had magic weapons at his disposal. He immediately employed them against the magic powers that emanated from Salva's flying vehicle. Pradyumna and his heroes dealt terrible destruction among the adversaries' forces. Thousands of war chariots were destroyed, and thousands of elephants were killed. But there was still the terrible flying vehicle from which Salva carried out his assaults. This flying vehicle was so mysterious that sometimes one imagined one could see several flying vehicles at once in the sky, and then believed that none was present at all. It was intermittently visible and invisible. The warriors of the Yadu dynasty were very confused because they kept seeing the strange flying vehicle appear in different places. Sometimes it appeared to be on the ground, then it appeared in the sky, then it seemed to rest briefly on the top of a mountain only to reappear on the surface of water. The wondrous vehicle moved in the sky like a firefly in the wind but never remained for very long in one place. In spite of these maneuvers, the warriors of the Yadu dynasty would pounce on the flying vehicle as soon as they caught sight of it. The warriors' darts shone like the Sun and were as dangerous as serpents' tongues.

The battle lasted twenty-seven days. At the time, Krishna, who had taken on the form of a human being, was staying with a king. He heard about the battle while he was there, and he knew that Salva wanted to kill him. Using his own celestial vehicle, Krishna flew to the city of Dwarka and saw the catastrophe that had taken place. He immediately turned to his own pilot, Daruka, and commanded, "Quickly take me to Salva. Even though he is mighty and mysterious, you need not be in the least afraid of him." Krishna's battle vehicle bore a flag with a picture of Garuda. Salva noticed Krishna approaching and released a mighty missile against him that flew through the air with a noise like thunder. It shone with such brilliance that it lit up the whole sky. Krishna, however, fired a counter missile, which caused Salva's missile to be broken up into a thousand pieces. Then he showered Salva's celestial city with a veritable flood of darts just as the Sun floods the entire sky with countless light particles on a clear day.

Salva would still not admit defeat and projected a number of illusions into the sky. Krishna, however, saw through this ruse. Undeterred by all the magic tricks, he located Salva's celestial vehicle and let off salvos of tongues of fire against him. Salva's passion for battle resembled the passion of flyers who plunge right into the adversary's fire. Krishna shot off so many darts with such unbelievable force that Salva's armor was torn apart, and his gem-encrusted helmet broke into a thousand pieces. Then Krishna shattered Salva's wonderful flying vehicle with an almighty blow, and countless pieces of debris fell down into the sea. Salva managed to get on to land before his flying vehicle hit the water, but Krishna lifted his wondrous fire wheel that shone with brilliance like the

Sun. When this happened, Krishna resembled the red Sun as it rises above a mountain. At the same moment, Salva was decapitated by the fire wheel, and his head, together with his earrings and the rest of his helmet, fell to the ground. Now Salva's soldiers set up a spine-chilling wailing and lamenting. Then the demi-gods arrived in their flying vehicles and caused flowers from different celestial planets to rain down onto the battlefield. A little later, Krishna visited the planet Sutala and the ruler there "sank down in an ocean of joy."

This is an eerie scene. Ray weapons, weapons of illusion, anti-missile missiles, and climate-altering weapons are described, as well as celestial structures that are able to change their positions within the shortest spaces of time. After reading texts like that, I always ask myself what our science-fiction authors are going to come up with next.

Inevitably, the question must be raised as to what happened to the remains of these weapons. If some of the wars that are maintained to have happened in the Indian texts really occurred, where is the debris? Where are the pieces of crashed celestial vehicles? Where are the remains of the bunkers of the defendants? Where are the remains of the ray cannons that shot the glowing darts into space with unbelievable force?

A cross-question: where are the remains of the thousands of tanks and aircraft from the Second World War? It is barely eighty years since that war and you will hardly find anything except what is displayed in museums. The battles in ancient India happened thousands of years ago—when exactly, nobody knows. Also, we have graphic descriptions of how entire countries were laid to waste and ashes, how even ray guns were employed and smashed celestial cities were plunged into the oceans. Who could successfully retrieve any trace of this? And when inexplicable objects are sometimes found—and I know of some—those pompous souls deposit them somewhere with great dignity under a mantle of secretiveness. I am still convinced, however, that we will discover the traces of space battles very soon. Certainly, on the Moon, in the asteroid belt, and on Mars. On Earth too if we look hard enough. This search has already begun, and it has been successful.

The preceding story centered on Dwarka, which was attacked from the air by the evil Salva. The same story, in a slightly different form, appears also in the Mahabharata (in the chapters on Sabha, Parva, Bhishma Parva, and Mausala Parva). It is always about the destruction of the city of Dwarka. Did this place ever exist?

For decades, Indian archaeologists have been asking themselves the same question—and have struck lucky. Just as Heinrich Schliemann believed in the stories by Homer, Indian scholars believe in the reports in the Mahabharata. Quite useable clues are given to the geographical location of Dwarka and, after years of painstaking research, have led to a result. The city described once lay on the (present) gulf of Kutsh (between Bombay [now called Mumbai] and Karachi, exactly at Lat. 22° 14" E, Long. 68° 58" N). Much as in Troy (in present-day Turkey), the excavators found eight layers at Dwarka, one above the other, with the little modern town, which was built in the sixteenth century, above the older ruins. At low tide, walls can be seen leading into the sea. These remains caused the experts to explore there too, by underwater archaeology. First, underwater cameras were used; then magnetometer measurements were made, after which underwater metal detectors were employed. While the Western media were reporting on underwater finds in the Mediterranean off Alexandria, the Indians—far away from the general media hype—were discovering the city Dwarka mentioned in the Mahabharata. First, the cameras began to capture pictures of artificially worked blocks of stone, "which excluded any possibility of natural transport on account of their size,"[34] such as might have occurred by underwater currents or the tides. Then walls were found that met at right angles to each other, streets and the outlines of former buildings, of temples and palaces of a once "high civilization"— this according to statements in a scientific report on Dwarka. Finally, there were finds of nails containing iron with silicon and magnesium components. "There is no doubt that further metal alloy objects must lie on the bed of the sea at Dwarka." This assumption is based on results from metal detectors. The scientific report on the finds, which were found up to several hundred meters from the coast, ends with the following words: "The clues in the Mahabharata about Dwarka as a city were neither exaggerations nor myths. It was a reality in the fullest meaning of the term."[35]

Indian geologists who participated in the exploration of the underwater ruins of Dwarka came face to face with remains of walls that displayed traces of vitrified stone. Stone will not melt unless extremely high temperatures are applied. This kind of vitrified stone is found not only in Dwarka but elsewhere too. There have never been any sensible explanations for the causes. As early as 1932, Patrick Clayton, a geologist employed by the Egyptian government, found puzzling greenish shining vitrified sand in the dunes of the "Great Sand Lake" (Saad Plateau, north of the south-western tip of Egypt). In July 1999, the British periodical *New Scientist* reported on vitrified sand in the Libyan Desert.[36] No volcanoes exist there, which might have been cited as the cause of these features. The Bedouins have always fashioned knives and axe heads out of this "desert glass." More than 1,000 tons of the desert glass have been found so far, without there being a convincing argument for its origin.

Even in the nineteenth century, reports about inexplicable vitrification haunted the press. In 1881, the *American Journal of Science* reported on the occasional vitrified granite block that had been discovered in French castles of the towns of Chateau-vieux and Puy de Gaude (northern coast).[37] In his book *Technology of the Gods*, American author David Hatcher Childress listed twenty-two places in the world where unexplained sand and stone vitrification can be observed.[38] I myself have seen a few places with vitrifications above the Peruvian city Cuzco. The riddle has never been solved, but it has also been pushed aside.

And now? This is just the beginning of a search with modern instruments. It has been known for decades that the rate of instances of cancer is much higher than the Indian average in the region around Jodhpur (Rajasthan, India). Unnatural mutations have been observed in birds in the region. It was not until 1999 that Indian scientists had the absurd idea of using detectors to check radioactivity, although there was neither a nuclear power station in the area nor had nuclear tests been carried out. The Geiger counters provided unexpected results. Layers of ash under the sand and stone clearly demonstrated measurable high rates of radioactivity. Where did it come from?

The Russian periodical *Trud* reported on June 24, 2000, about Professor Ernest Muldaschew's expedition undertaken in the Tibetan-Nepalese border area. There, Tibetan monks had told him about the ruins of a city that had been built by the gods. The place was situated near the holy mountain Kailas. I am only repeating this story with reservations because I could not check the source. Maybe an expedition will one day set out to this mountainous area, in which—at least I can confirm this—exist wondrous traditions about those gods who, many thousands of years ago, were active as teachers of humankind.

So where does our path lead? Right into the deepest past of humankind. Into a prehistoric period, in which we do not want to believe, as our eyes and common sense have been gummed up with the sanctified theory of evolution.

Although some progress has been reported in Chinese archaeology over the past few decades, China's ancient history still remains a mystery. The little that has been discovered clearly points to those mystical "ancient emperors" who once came from the sky on flying dragons. Rulers and priests in this "Kingdom of the Center" have for thousands of years considered themselves to be the representatives of the only and highest civilization of Earth because they believe that they received their teachings, their technologies, and their astronomical knowledge directly from the gods. Reports in Chinese monasteries tell of the *san huang*, the "three exalted ones," and the *wu di*, the "five original emperors." These figures are not historically traceable.

Written history begins with Yu, as the hereditary succession on the Chinese throne began with him. Yu is supposed to have been active sometime between the twenty-first and sixteenth centuries BC. Naturally, he was looked upon as a divine being, and the same was true for Yu's successors for a long time. Even 1,000 years later, the Chinese looked upon their ruler, "the great Yu" (Zhou period, eleventh century BC to 771 BC) as a divine being who had lifted the land out of floods of water. Long before the great Yu, there were the Xia and Shang dynasties, which have always been categorized as mystical and not real by archaeologists, until a sudden find of so-called oracles bones. These bones provided the names of twenty-three rulers that were deciphered and found unambiguously to belong to the Shang dynasty. A total of some 100,000 inscribed bones turned up in subterranean installations near Xiaotun (in the north of the Henan Province). Originally, there must have been far more, because the local inhabitants had been grinding the bones to powder as healing agents for hundreds of years. An entire library of bones. At present, only about a third of them have been deciphered because the inscriptions on the bones encompass an alphabet of some 3,000 signs. That long ago!

In the eleventh century BC, the last Shang ruler was defeated by the Zhou, and one would think that the cult surrounding divine rulers would have ceased at this point. Wrong—it had only just begun. The Zhou rulers lived according to the rules of *tianming*, the Mandate of Heaven. Heaven,

Chinese *tian*, was firmly anchored in the heads of the priests and rulers. Every ruler was called *tianzi*—Son of Heaven. Rulers who did not live and reign in accordance with the concept of *tianming* could not be genuine sons of Heaven and were, therefore, deposed or killed.

Who would be surprised to learn, then, that all the Chinese rulers from the very earliest times (nobody knows how far back) had to carry out certain ceremonies at an "altar of Heaven" and had to speak to the old gods? The rulers were seen as intermediaries between Earth and the celestial powers, and they saw themselves, without exception, as "sons of Heaven." To this day, two of these "altars of Heaven" are still known—one in Beijing and a second one, only recently excavated, in the city of Xian. This "altar of Heaven" is a round structure consisting of four platforms superimposed one above the other, with a fifth platform in the center. Each of these platforms lies about one meter higher than the one underneath. Cross-walls that lead from the top to the bottom divide the platforms into twelve different stages—as for the ancient Chinese, the number twelve signifies the division of the heavens into twelve parts.

And what has all this to do with India and Central America or with vimanas driven by mercury? In Peru, the Inca rulers and, naturally, their ancestors also looked upon themselves as "sons of Heaven" (as did the Japanese, the Persian, and the Ethiopian imperial houses). The "sons of Heaven" in Peru also carried out their ceremonies and conversations with the divine ancestors on an "altar of Heaven." One of these altars lies above the Peruvian city of Cuzco, almost right above the puzzling ruins of the fortress of

Sacsayhuaman. It has the same structure as the "altars of Heaven" in China, except they are halfway around the world apart from each other! Who took on what from whom? Or who influenced whom?

Vitrified stone is found in many places above the Inca fortress at Sacsayhuaman (Peru).

"Altars of Heaven," which are 25,000 thousand kilometers apart by air.

Whenever I study archaeological, ethnological, or religious-philosophical works—and this happens every week during my work—I can never quite shake off the feeling that I am stumbling about in the dark because nothing fundamentally new ever turns up in these works. It is essentially hideously boring literature, written by similar-thinking people for similar-thinking people. They all behave as though they had been programmed the same way, like unconscious beings twitching in time with each other. I have ceased to be surprised about this, as I know how the system works. No real cross-referencing occurs outside of their learned subjects because it is not known.

I maintain that at least some of the weapons described in the ancient Indian traditions really existed and were employed—as were the vimanas and the celestial cities. However, it should not be up to just me and a few like-minded people to produce the proof for these assertions. Neither I nor my colleagues have an institution at our disposal that would be financially in a position to supply experts with the necessary means to address very specific questions. Underwater archaeology is very expensive, aerial archaeology no less so. In the meantime, ruins can be located as deep as 25 meters in the ground, with the help of synthetic aperture radar (SAR). This is done by emitting microwaves in the P-band range from a height of about 3,000 meters. They are at frequency ranges of between 380 and 450 megahertz. The microwaves penetrate deep into the ground and are reflected. Even objects that are only 30 centimeters long can be made visible with the SAR system. This kind of archaeological sounding is very expensive, of course. India cannot afford it. And afterward one would have to follow up the results; the finds would have to be analyzed. If such technology were to be employed in researching the ancient city of Dwarka, I am sure we would soon come upon traces of former weapons systems as they are mentioned in the Mahabharata.

What should we do? All I can do is point out those cross-references and beg the scholars to become active in this or that direction. If space wars have taken place, it should be possible today to find traces of them, somewhere on Earth, buried under thick sand and soil layers, somewhere in the oceans, covered over by mountains of coral. We are not lacking in technological aids to carry out such a first step. The finer work could be done later—I have a host of precise questions about selected geographical locations. I cannot go to the Moon, even less to Mars, although even there, the present-day results of measurements taken by space probes have turned up quite a few inexplicable things.

As far back as July 31, 1976, the American Mars probes (Viking Project) photographed curious shapes on the surface of Mars, which became the starting point for speculation and a number of theories.[39] A face was seen in the Cydonia region of Mars (Viking photo 35A72). Rectangular structures that resembled artificially made walls (Viking photo No. 86A10) and even structures resembling pyramids were seen on the surface of Mars (Mariner 9 photos Nos. 4205–78 and, even more precise, Viking photos 35A72, 70A13, and 70A11). It goes without saying that these curious formations were ascribed to natural causes, and twenty years later, NASA photos no longer produced the face on Mars. The riddle was filed away. Too early, in my opinion. Although no face on Mars existed on the later pictures, one was able to see a giant ellipse of rock in the position where the face once was. The wall-like rectangular structures were still there, and the triangular form of a pyramid survived. In the meantime, the first organic traces turned up in Martian rock, and NASA announced that water, although in a frozen state, should exist under the surface of Mars.[40] This points to former activity on Mars.

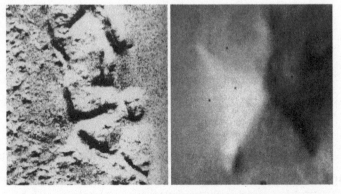

Rectangular structures and a pyramidal shape on Mars.

The old question regarding what is not right about the two moons of Mars is still unanswered. They are called Phobos and Deimos (fear and terror). They were already known before American astronomer Asaph Hall discovered the moons in 1877. In 1610 Johannes Kepler suspected that Mars was accompanied by two satellites. What is really astonishing, however, is the narrative that appears in Jonathan Swift's 1726 book, *Gulliver's Travels,* in a chapter about a journey to Laputa. Not only did he describe the two moons, he even knew their size and orbits. In the third chapter, we find the following:

> *They [the Laputan astronomers] spend the greatest Part of their Lives in observing the celestial Bodies, which they do by the Assistance of Glasses, far excelling ours in Goodness. For, although their largest Telescopes do not exceed three Feet, they magnify much more than those of a Hundred with us, and shew the Stars with greater Clearness. This Advantage hath enabled them to extend their Discoveries much farther than our Astronomers in Europe. They have made a Catalogue of ten Thousand fixed Stars, whereas the largest of ours do not contain above one third Part of that Number. They have likewise discovered two lesser Stars, or Satellites, which revolve about Mars; whereof the innermost is distant from the Center of the primary Planet exactly three of his Diameters and the outermost five; the former revolves in the Space of ten Hours, and the latter in Twenty-one and a Half; so that the Squares of their periodical Times, are very near in the same Proportion with the Cubes of their Distance from the Center of Mars . . .[41]*

How was Jonathan Swift able to describe these moons if they were only discovered 150 years later? It is a fact that these satellites are the smallest and most peculiar moons in our solar system; they move in almost circular orbits around the equator of Mars. Phobos and Deimos are the only moons in our solar system so far known to move faster around the mother planet than the planet itself revolves. Taking into account the rotation of Mars, Phobos manages two orbits in one Martian day, while Deimos moves around Mars a little faster than Mars takes for a revolution around its own axis. The peculiar characteristics of Phobos do not stand in a proper relation to its apparent mass.

Naturally, one assumes the same history of creation of the Mars moons as for all other moons around other planets. It is believed they are fragments from space that have been captured by the gravitational field of Mars. This theory has one flaw: both of Mars's moons orbit the planet in almost the same plane above the Mars equator. One fragment may accidentally do this, but for two to do it, the theory that it is purely coincidental becomes rather tenuous. In the meantime, various satellites from Earth have peered at these Mars moons and sent back good photos to Earth. Both moons are "potato-shaped" fragments with various impact craters. Twice, attempts were made to fly above the Mars moons at a relatively close distance. None of the satellites from Earth attained its target. Our earthly probes "went blind" before they could transmit photos back to Earth. The earlier photos sent back to Earth by satellites have not cleared up the problem of the Mars moons. We now have "potatoes with craters," true, but we know as little about the inner life of these minute space bodies as we do about their peculiar orbits.

The question about the craters that pepper all the moons and planets in our solar system has never been answered satisfactorily. Admittedly, space debris constantly bombards the surfaces of planets that have no protective layer of air—which would at least cause the smaller fragments to burn up. But why are there so many craters? And why on such small moons like Phobos and Deimos? Those two really do not have the gravitational fields of large planets. One cannot help getting the impression that an unbelievably heavy barrage of asteroids once flew through our solar system. From where? What was the cause? We know that hundreds of thousands of these bits of space debris have accumulated between Mars and Jupiter in the so-called asteroid belt. Nobody knows the cause of this. Star Wars?

Here, too, humans have the technological means to pursue these questions, but nothing is done. Why? Because the "system" would think it was absurd to release funds for such projects.

The same state of affairs goes for the Moon, which is only 384,400 kilometers from us. Several NASA probes photographed "unexplained tectonic anomalies" there. One of them, in the Mare Crisium, resembles a kind of bridge. The endlessly diligent Luc Bürgin, who was the chief editor of a Basle newspaper, reported on this.[42] Another phenomenon, which can be observed from Earth itself with a halfway decent telescope, lies in the Mare Vaporum (for astronomers, 16.5° N and 4–6° E). A runway-like line stretches right through the Moon debris and even seems to cut through parts of rocks. The line terminates at both ends with a straight line and two right angles. Nature does not tend to produce lines like that, especially not across a stretch of 30 kilometers. We have missed something here so far because we do not want to know more. This will change because humans will eventually settle on the Moon and later on Mars. This is as certain as the Sun rising in the East. And this is why I am pleading for reason and a relaxation of attitudes: let us research these riddles and stop all the childish secretiveness.

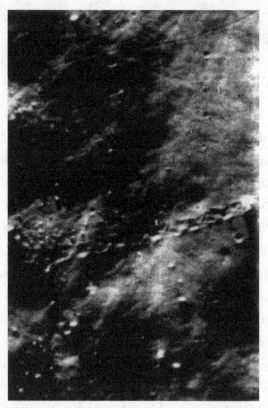

A runway-like structure on the surface of the
Moon stretches across debris.

No one has so far been able to explain this interwoven line
on the Moon's surface.

Based on the photos alone, I would consider it rather
adventurous to attempt geological dating with regard to the
Moon or Mars. Naturally, geologists know about the layer-
ing of rocks on Earth and how many million years it took
for certain formations to attain their present structures,
and naturally, insights based on conditions on Earth can
be transferred to other planets. But all this is not sufficient
to date, at a distance, rectangular shapes on the surface of
Mars, because although the surrounding rocks may be millions of years old, the artificial shapes need not be. It is rather
as if we were to photograph the Earth's surface from Mars
and were to discover something like a wall in a mountainous valley. Geologists would work out when the mountainous
valley would have had to have been created and would not
understand that the wall was really a dam. Conclusions are

drawn too quickly. With regard to the Moon or Mars, we shall obtain reliable data only if a human being or robot stands on the spot itself. A human being would be more reliable than a robot because a human being can make deductions and will notice details that may escape the robot's program.

A variety of geological dating methods exist on Earth, all of which have their shortcomings. The origins of the ancient texts themselves cannot be dated, even if we locate the oldest manuscript. Why not? Because we do not know how old the story was before somebody wrote it down for the first time. Indian astronomers have tried to reconstruct a date for the Mahabharata by studying any mention of astronomical information. Based on such references, this Indian epic could have been produced at any date between 6,000 and 3,000 BC,[43] perhaps even earlier.

A further problem arises through the different datings of various calendars. I have mentioned before that the Maya calendar—adapted to ours—gives a date of August 11, 3114 BC, for its inception.[44] Why? Because "the gods came down from the pathway of the stars" on that day. "They spoke the magic language of the stars in the sky."[45] That was 5,000 years ago, in a time we know nothing about, but that does not stop us from pretending we were there. Aymara Indians in the ruins of Tiahuanaco (Bolivia) celebrated the beginning of their calendar on March 21, 2000. The beginning was exactly 5,008 years before. In India, the Western calendar is officially used, but twenty different calendars appear in their religious traditions, all of which have different inception dates way back in the past. A Sirius calendar has been foisted on the ancient Egyptians, one that actually never existed, and the Jewish world religion starts its calendar with the creation of the world. That was on October 7, 3761 BC. Now, according to Jewish tradition, 1,000 years count as one day with God. This means that when the seventh millennium begins for the Jewish calendar, the seventh day begins for God. According to Jewish concepts, this is when the Messiah will come again.

I have previously discussed the fact that all peoples, whether extinct or not, are familiar with the concept of some kind of bringer of salvation.[46] We do not seem to be able to learn from this. How has that witty satirist among scientists, Professor Erwin Chargaff, phrased it:

> *The only thing we learn from history is that we learn nothing from history and—all this takes up thousands of pages.*[47]

Our knowledge of the past history of humankind is lousy. In former millennia, book burnings were organized by politicians and religious authorities in order that only one truth should prevail. Such acts of destruction, while rare, do continue to this day, yet the planet is teeming with books and millions of messages flit around the world via the internet. Not that it helps us much, as human beings will pick out only what they want. And even then, only a very small number of human beings can afford such things, compared with the nearly eight billion souls on our blue globe. Quo vadis, homo sapiens?

Several years ago, French astronomer Chantal Jègues-Wolkiewiez made some astonishing discoveries that have made a number of prehistorians very angry. Madame Jègues studied cave drawings in some depth, among them those in the cave of Lascaux in the French Dordogne. The cave drawings had been dated to about 17,000 years ago. Logically—the dogma of evolution does not allow anything else but logic—only primitive Stone Age people could have existed back then. In fact, the cave drawings do show horses, stags, bulls, curious lines and dots, all fashioned with the colors that were available in the Stone Age. Archaeology has only ever interpreted these cave drawings to mean little more than the needs of hunters of large game to decorate their caves. But the best of these decorated caves are not in locations where our Stone Age hunters would have lived, but miles away from them and always in areas that are difficult to access. Prehistorians have concluded from this that the caves served as assembly halls in which certain ceremonies were carried out, that they were probably places of importance for spirits or shamans—who have always been cited in connection with every kind of nonsense. Therefore, Stone Age people were presumed to have created prehistoric shrines—they were the churches of the Stone Age.

Madame Jègues discovered some quite different connections. As an astronomer, she noticed things that would not have occurred to archaeologists at all. The cave drawings actually depict stars and entire constellations that the Babylonians and Chaldeans had always been thought to have observed and named—much later! Here, we had the constellations of Scorpius, Aries the ram, Taurus the bull, the mountain goat Capricorn, and so on.

That these cave drawings could depict constellations could not be coincidence, as the insights gained by Madame Jègues are confirmed every year, both by astronomy and the position of the cave complex. Every year, at the summer solstice, the rays of the setting Sun shine down the cave entrance and illuminate the drawings in the Hall of the Bulls. Madame Jègues says, "This place was not chosen by coincidence. The drawings were created as part of a fantastic show, when the sun shines into and illuminates the entire Hall of the Bulls."[48]

First of all, this astronomer had made a map of the starry sky as it would have appeared to an observer 17,000 years ago. Then all the dots and lines of the animal figures were measured meticulously, and the results obtained were compared with a computer program of the night sky of 17,000 years ago. The correspondence between the two was exact. Astronomer Gérard Jasniewicz (University of Montpellier, France), who checked Madame Jègues's data, commented, "Several elements tally without any room for doubt. The alignment of the cave towards the summer solstice, the positioning of Capricorn, Scorpius and Taurus in the hall correspond with the sky at that time."[49] What does the science of prehistory have to say to all this? "Pure speculation," according to Dr. Harold Floss of the University of Tübingen.

Nothing new under the Sun. Things cannot be that cannot be. Astronomers in the Stone Age just do not fit into the framework of evolution, the only framework that makes us happy. Cave dwellers have to be primitive; they may hunt big game, scrape furs, look for berries, and carve spears. They may be prototypical, and are allowed to have smeared simple drawings onto the cave walls, but they are not allowed to have been capable of abstract thought and definitely could not have known exact astronomy. There was a lot of rain 17,000 years ago, and the sky could not be observed all year round, so how could the Stone Age hunter have studied astronomy? In addition to which, these fur-clad dolts would not have had the time, anyway. They had to hunt mammoths, defend themselves against bears, protect their families, and keep the fire going. There was no time left for astronomy of a higher kind.

So, how could this have been? Let us assume, for a moment, that the battles described in the Mahabharata with all those space weapons of the gods (radioactivity . . . vitrified sand and rocks!) really had happened and the survivors of that terrible epoch had been thrown back to the Stone Age. They had nothing left: no libraries, no metal tools, no pleasure gardens or swimming pools, not even fabric or writing tools. Even the most necessary things of everyday life had to be created all over again. The weapons of the gods had done their work efficiently. This is not such an absurd scenario; it can be read again in the works of the philosopher Plato, as I have noted before.[50] In spite of the catastrophe, the survivors still had one thing: their knowledge. This they passed on verbally to the next generation and tried to depict things they considered important with the means at hand, such as the home of the gods, the locations in the sky.

Today, nobody who is familiar with the material can dispute that all the Stone Age peoples were quite crazy about astronomy. In the area around the Gulf of Morbihan alone (Brittany, France), 135 out of a total of 156 dolmens are aligned on the summer or winter solstices.[51] Stonehenge, in England, has proven to be a great observatory that made possible a whole chain of astronomical predictions. The prehistoric builders had observed the paths of many stars like Capella, Castor and Pollux, Vega, Antares, Altair or Deneb.[52]

Even German astronomers found out, after some delay, that the Stone Age folk of Stonehenge were able to predict all the solar and lunar eclipses.[53] And if one can believe the official dating (about which I have my doubts, for good reasons), long before Stonehenge (more than 5,000 years ago), our fur-clad Stone Age brothers built their gigantic journeyman's piece at Newgrange in Ireland, astronomically aligned, of course—how could it have been otherwise?[54, 55]

The only question is: *why* should these Stone Age people, who had hardly come down from the trees, be so obsessed with astronomy? This is something the experts cannot agree on.

All of the peculiar things that I have touched on here *do exist*. The details of all these matters are publicly accessible, whether in books, on the internet, or in specialist periodicals. But nobody draws conclusions from them. Has human society become lethargic? Has that inner urge of curiosity dried up? Are we simply overfed with information? Would we rather slouch in front of the television or the computer screen instead of crawling about outside? What good is this increase in knowledge in our electronic age if we do nothing with it? Our youth fiddle about with smartphones and play online games; color screens bombard our retinas with pictures and data that are immediately forgotten again. We "surf" over information but do not "dive" into it.

More than thirty years ago, I reported on a 5,000-year-old tool factory that exists not far from the Dutch village of Rijckholt, between Aachen and Maastricht, but that does not fit into our picture of Stone Age people. When I visited this place in the summer of 1998, I was only able to find out that the branch of science relevant to the find was not interested in this prehistoric flint mine. It is pushed away and forgotten. Television has never bothered to become involved in this fascinating riddle, and the most the experts can do is to pluck at their Woodstock-era beards and know nothing. It is a mystery to me what they spend their time reading.

So, what of the old mine? I wrote about it in some detail in my book, *Die Steinzeit war ganz anders.*[56] Here is a brief resumé:

During the 1920s, monks in the Dominican monastery of Rijckholt discovered shafts in the ground, from which they eventually brought 1,200 flint axes to the surface. Members of the Dutch Geological Society managed to rummage around and come up with sixty-six mine shafts during the 1960s, but a few thousand more are suspected. The number and size of the mine shafts gave rise to estimates that some 41,250 cubic meters of flint core pieces must have been extracted during the Stone Age. This would have yielded a production of some 153 million axes! In these shafts, 15,000 tools were located, and conservative estimates indicated that some two and half million of these Stone Age tools must still be lying about in the ground. If one assumes that the mine had been worked for, say, 500 years, a daily output of some 1,500 axes would have been produced. And all of this was more or less exactly 5,180 years ago.

It is well known that Stone Age hunters used flints for all kinds of purposes. Flint core lumps are found in chalk strata from the Cretaceous Period. Nature releases flint lumps when the chalk mantle dissolves through the action of erosion and weathering. So far, so good. This kind of dissolution rarely happens on the surface, and definitely not in Rijckholt. So who instructed our Stone Age folk, who were not members of unions, that a layer of flint was to be found deep in the ground, under a layer of sand, gravel, and chalk? Who organized the building of mine shafts? Removing one cubic meter of chalk would have cost about seven broken stone axes. Who "sold" these huge quantities of the stuff? Where did the goods go? What routes were used? What chief or boss organized the whole thing? Is there something situated in the proximity for which one would require thousands upon thousands of stone axes? A figure of at least 1,500 axes per day is not chickenfeed.

I do not know the answers, but the world of experts should be interested in it. They seem not to care. Young archaeologists who are spoilt by the internet do not go on digging expeditions. This flint mine, with all its accompanying paraphernalia, does not fit into our concept of Stone Age people, which prehistorians have been spoonfeeding us for decades. This is the way things go in the Western world. But it is different in the Asiatic sphere. There, although the basic concept of evolution is scientifically anchored (one thing arises from another), people think in very different passages of time than they do in the dominating West. Passages of time are also elements of religion, which is why no Indian scholar has any quarrel with the *yugas* (enormously long periods of time). Perhaps mankind has indeed become human from ape-like ancestors on the evolutionary path, but some circumstances or other—possibly wars with divine weapons—have thrown humans back into the Stone Age, and they had to dust themselves down and start all over again. Or genetic intervention by the gods (classical and ancient literature is full of artificially created human beings) gave humans an evolutionary shove into the future.

The Asiatic world thinks in terms of very different passages of time because the religious traditions are a component of thought in those societies. These traditions, even if they were renewed over and over again, were turned to stone in temples and sculptures. All the Indian temples are copies of those celestial habitations of the gods who once followed their courses across the heavens. Celestial vehicles turned to stone. The Temple of Konarak in the Indian province of Orissa, which has now been added to the UNESCO list of protected monuments in the world, served as a landmark for centuries for sea-going ships heading for Calcutta. The pagoda points to the sky, black as a raven. Only when they were on land would the sea travelers have noticed that the entire temple complex resembled one giant celestial vehicle, with a total of twenty-four wheels around it. Naturally, the structure is aligned astronomically, and it goes without saying that it is woven in with the calendar. The temple is supposed to be a copy of the vehicle that Indra once used to fly through the sky. This is nothing out of the ordinary in India. All the temples are celestial vehicles, and the top of every temple is crowned with some kind of vimana, those smaller flying vehicles in which human beings and gods flew in the sky and in space in those times. They and/or their descendants could just as well have turned up in the Peruvian desert of Nazca, or could have had huge quantities of flints scraped out of the ground in present-day Rijckholt, for whatever reasons, if they had had a mind to. Nothing would have prevented them from doing so. The gods and the demigods were mighty, and the humans whom they ripped off did everything for them.

The gods were supposed to have used certain weapons? So the masons and plasterers tried to copy them (which they never managed to do!). Scientific studies exist on this,[57] which nobody in the West is interested in. The gods and certain selected humans had disposed of secret weapons, it says in the ancient Indian texts. Has anything changed regarding this? Since Francis Bacon observed in the sixteenth century that knowledge is power: every group tries to preserve its knowledge in secret—as long as they can. Encoded messages, secret technologies, insider knowledge, and the like did not exist only in the past. Today it still exists—more than ever. "Secret knowledge is power."[58] Climate-altering weapons are mentioned in the Indian texts. Impossible? The American military researched such a weapon. Where? North of the little town of Gakona, Alaska. The project was called HAARP (High Frequency Active Auroral Research Program). If fully developed, HAARP would have been able to cut proper holes in the sky and make targeted alterations to the climate. Nothing new on God's earth.

India's gods are supposed to have chosen individual human beings and smaller groups to be their servants, from whom the royal houses were then derived. Is this nothing but a disguised form of racism? And what about that business with the ancient Israelites who considered themselves to be the chosen people? This still applies today, and within the huge Jewish family of belief, some consider themselves to be more chosen than others. Perhaps they are. The descendants of the Jewish high priests—those from the house of the Levites who were specially educated and looked after the ark of the covenant—are the present-day Cohenim. Approximately 5 percent of the world population of male Jews belong to this group, and they all actually carry the same genetic markers on certain parts of their Y-chromosomes. Jerusalem rabbi Jakob Kleinman said of this, "The genes prove that God keeps his promise: we will not be lost."[59]

Nothing is lost, and gradually the old truths see the light of day again. Insofar as they are allowed to be published.

Until not so long ago, astronomers taught that our Earth had a unique position in the universe. The argument went that the location of our Earth was simply a lucky one-off, as the Earth orbits the Sun at the ideal distance: not too warm and not too cold. Only because of this could life evolve in the way it has. This theory has been scrapped. British astronomer Sir Martin Rees, a professor at King's College Cambridge, publicly admitted, "Planetary systems are so common in our galaxy, that Earth-like planets probably occur in their millions."[60] It has taken years to support this conclusion, but it will take many decades until totalitarian religious communities are allowed to learn this. "The final goal of every censure is only to allow books which nobody reads anyway" (Giovanni Guareschi).

Afterthoughts

Clever people may pretend to be stupid; the reverse
is much more difficult.
—KURT TUCHOLSKY

I HAVE BEEN MOCKING the theory of evolution ever since
I started writing books. And I do this even though I know that
all forms of life are subject to the laws of evolution. I never
set out to question the basic direction of evolution. The only
thing is that evolution has not run in a straight line but leap-
frogs in two directions. On the one hand, genetic messages
are constantly fed into the "Earth system." They reach us via
cosmic dust. On the other hand, extraterrestrials make targeted interventions in the human genome. As is asserted in
the traditions of humankind, the gods created humans "in
their image." Genetic material has been inserted into our evolutionary process. I will not repeat again here why I have been
representing the case for this concept for more than fifty-five
years.

Year after year, anthropology serves up contradictory data about our ancestors. Hardly has a new skull turned up than we are being presented with the very newest, up-to-date pre-human. A constant process of squabbling. No sooner had we got used to the Out-of-Africa theory—according to which the first representatives of Homo sapiens set off out of Africa about 100,000 years ago to populate the Earth—than Out-of-Africa is seen in relative terms. "The more we know, the more bewildering the picture becomes," said American scientist David Mann.[1] This bewilderment is only going to increase.

In 1973, for the first time, a virus gene was successfully introduced into a bacterium. In 1978, the synthetic variant of the human insulin gene was transplanted into an E. choli bacterium. In 1981, the first transgenic mammals followed: seven mice. In 1988, the Harvard cancer mouse was presented to a flabbergasted humankind; a year later, transgene sheep and goats followed, and shortly afterward, the transgene cow. In between, human sperm donation and artificial fertilization became routine and the first test-tube babies were born. Botanists, not inactive, began manipulating the genes of plants. Then came the cloned mice, sheep, and cattle. The next items to be created according to designer genes were mixed beings, and when I wrote these lines, I had just read about another trick of geneticists—the first genetically altered primates.[2] Scientists at the University of Portland (USA) gave the little monkey the sweetest name: ANDi (*DNA* reversed with an *I* on the end).

As always, these developments are commented on in magazines and on TV shows, and groups of people who have not the foggiest idea what it is all about start interfering. In principle, this is a good thing in a democracy. A great deal is talked about ethics and morals, and that human beings should not play God. There is a final boundary (I heard this said by level-headed theologians) that God would not countenance. Only one person understood this and even spoke it out loud: British physicist Stephen Hawking. In front of a large audience in Mumbai, he observed that gene technology would one day create new humans who were cleverer and more resilient than the present humans.[3]

All efforts and all laws passed would not alter a thing about this. Hawking's statement was not even original. What is approaching humanity in terms of genetic innovations is old hat. It existed thousands of years ago and can be read in the literature of our forefathers. Many traditions report on genetic manipulation of the human genome, on targeted artificial mutations, and naturally also on chimera, those mixed beings of mythology.

The ancient interventions were all by the gods. They were "changing the points." One may argue about the reasons why they did this, but very soon no longer about the fact that *it happened*. Why not? Deoxyribonucleic acid (DNA), the ancestral material of our genes, has been decoded and transparent man has arrived. In spite of the decoding of the complete human genome, the task has not ended here. We now know the pages of the book, so to speak, but not yet the individual phrases and words. Forty years ago, when I wrote about the decoding of the human genome, I earned ridicule and rejection. This would never be possible, I was told, with all those billions of possibilities that lay in DNA; if it was ever to be, then it might possibly come about in 1,000 years. And what now? The family tree of human beings is contained in the genetic message, and our geneticists, with their unbelievable technological possibilities, are too clever to overlook this fact. In a few years' time, they will discover that certain sequences in this design cannot be the outcome of the evolutionary process. They will find that there were something like ancient parents (Adam and Eve), but not just one pair. They will find out that "somebody" has been manipulating our genes, and they will—whether they want to or not—have to ask who might be responsible for this. The answer has been lying on the table before the question was even asked: the gods. The next arguments will be about what kind of gods, and finally will follow the entire catalogue of questions that like-minded people and I have been dealing with for decades. Will we then have reached the end of science, the end of history or the end of religions? No.

Two powers control human thinking: science and religion. They move on different paths, but both have the same departure point and the same goal. The cause? Curiosity. The goal? Knowledge. All our doing and thinking is about science and religion. What has faith to do with research? What has scientific insight to do with faith? A church that ignores the secure scientific insights is dogmatic and will not be able to survive in a planetary society. Self-righteousness cannot go with science. And a science that ignores awe and the inner voice of religious feelings will find it hard to exist as we, the religious ones and the scientific ones, all live in the same world. The religious side may delay scientific research. This often happened in the past. Are questions of faith and theology fundamentally different from questions of science? In the end, probably not—both are searching for a final truth. The paths to knowledge vary. A monk in his monastery may arrive at the same results about God and the creation of the universe as the astrophysicist. The difference is that the astrophysicist can prove his knowledge; the monk is given his. His knowledge has to be believed. Research has uncovered a connection between human good health and mental attitude. Statistics show that optimistic people become ill with cancer less often than depressive people. A human being is a psychosomatic unit. Now, neurological studies explain what is taking place in our "neurotransmitter," the brain, and we can even make visible those electric impulses in the brain. But we do not know how they arise. Science and religion are working in the same human being. What is this spirit inside us that makes possible imagination, curiosity, and even causes healing?

Humans have tried to broaden their horizons with all kinds of drugs. They have experienced a different world in an LSD-induced trance. But this other world was really the same as before, only the senses and, therefore, perceptions had changed. To this day, not a single scientific insight has resulted from this mind-altering pill. So where does the spirit come from? This is both a scientific and a theological question. Science gives answers to questions on the Big Bang or Big Bangs, on black holes, and on the expansion of the universe. Religious philosophers would like to know whether we are alone in the universe and whether creation only happened because of humankind. Only science can provide answers to those questions. And if science finds out that we are not alone in the universe, this will in no way mean the end of religion, but its continuation. What theological insights have the extraterrestrials arrived at? Based on what scientific data? Science and religion are actually compatible, just so long as religion is not dogmatic. Is there an intelligent designer behind the cosmos? Is God the first (and last) source for our whole behavior? Even for our scientific curiosity?

One thing is certain: religion cannot disconnect itself from scientific insights. The laws of gravitation do not adhere to religious or cultural boundaries. Crusades in the name of religion can no longer be carried out. (We will have to live for a while longer with restrained self-righteousness.) What remains is respectful coexistence of the two forces of science and religion. The shadows of fundamentalism are still hanging over humankind. The task of religion and science is to chase away these shadows with the peaceful weapons of the human spirit.

NOTES

INTRODUCTION

1. Ruegg, Walter (publisher), *Die Ägyptische Götterwelt* [*The Egyptian World of the Gods*], Zurich and Stuttgart, 1959.

2. Blavatsky, Helena P., *The Secret Doctrine*, Vol. 1, London, 1888.

3. von Däniken, Erich, *Im Namen von Zeus*, Munich, 1999. [Available in English as *Odyssey of the Gods*, Chrysalis Vega, London, 2002.]

4. White, John, *Ancient History of the Maori*, Vol. I–II, Wellington, 1887.

5. Roy, Potrap Chandra, *The Mahabharata*, Drona Parva, Calcutta, 1888.

6. Berdyczewski, M. J. (Bin Gorion), *Die Sagen der Juden von der Urzeit* [*Legends of the Jews from Ancient Times*], Frankfurt a. M., 1913.

7. Gundert, Wilhelm, *Japanische Religionsgeschichte* [*A Japanese History of Religion*], Stuttgart, 1936.

8. von Däniken, Erich, *Der Götterschock* [Not available in English], Munich, 1992.

CHAPTER 1

1. Plato, *Timaeus*. English translation by H. D. P. Lee, Penguin, 1971.

2. Kautzsch, Emil, *Die Apokryphen und Pseudepigraphen des Alten Testaments* [*The Apocrypha and Pseudo-epigraphs of the Old Testament*, Fourth Book Esra], Hildesheim, 1962.

3. von Däniken, Erich, *Im Namen von Zeus*, Munich, 1999. [Available in English as *Odyssey of the Gods*, Chrysalis Vega, London, 2002.]

4. von Däniken, Erich, *Der Götterschock* [Not available in English], Munich, 1992.

5. Rahner, Karl, *Herders Theologisches Lexicon* [*Herders' Theological Encyclopedia*, Vol. I], Freiburg, Basel, Vienna, 1972.

6. Rahner, *Herders Theologisches Lexicon*.

7. Pritchard, James B., *Near Eastern Texts Relating to the Old Testament*, London, 1972.

8. Burckhardt, Georg, *Gilgamesch. Eine Erzählung aus dem alten Orient*, Wiesbaden, 1958. [The following alternative translation is currently available—Temple, Robert, *He Who Saw Everything. A Verse Translation of the Epic of Gilgamesh*, Rider, London, 1991.]

9. Burckhardt, *Gilgamesch. Eine Erzählung aus dem alten Orient*.

10. Burckhardt, *Gilgamesch. Eine Erzählung aus dem alten Orient*.

11. Lambert, Wilfried G., and Millard, Alan R., *Atra Hasis. The Babylonian Story of the Flood*, Oxford, 1970.

12. *Der Midrasch Bereschit Rabba,* übersetzt von A. Wünsche [*The Midrash Bereshit Rabba,* translated into German by A. Wünsche], Leipzig, 1881.

13. *Der Midrasch Schemit Rabba.*

14. Roy, Chandra Protap, *The Mahabharata, Musala Parva,* Vol. IX, Calcutta, 1896.

15. *The Jewish Encyclopedia,* "Aaron," New York, London, 1906.

16. Ginzberg, Louis, *The Legends of the Jews,* Vol. III, Philadelphia, 1968.

17. Sassoon, George, and Dale, Rodney, "Deus est machina?," in *New Scientist,* April 1976.

18. Sassoon, George, and Dale, Rodney, *The Manna Machine,* London, 1978.

19. *Kebra Negest, 1. Abt., Die Herrlichkeit der Könige. Abhandlungen der Philosophisch-Philologischen Klasse der Königlich Bayerischen Akademie der Wissenschaften,* Bd. 23. [*Kebra Negest, 1st section, The Splendor of the Kings. Treatises by the Philosophical-Philological Class of the Royal Bavarian Academy of Sciences,* Vol. 23].

20. Schmitt, Rainer, *Zelt und Lade als Thema alttestamentlicher Wissenschaft* [*The Tent and the Ark of the Covenant as Subjects of Old Science*], Gütersloh, 1972.

21. Dibelius, Martin, *Die Lade Jahves—eine religions-geschichtliche Untersuchung* [*The Ark of Jehovah—A Religious-Historical Investigation*], Göttingen, 1906.

22. Vatke, R., *Die biblische Theologie—wissenschaftlich dargestellt* [*Biblical Theology—Scientifically Presented*], Berlin, 1835.

23. Torczyner, Harry, *Die Bundeslade und die Anfänge der Religion Israels* [*The Ark of the Covenant and the Beginnings of the Religion of Israel*], 1930.

24. Eissfeldt, Otto, *Einleitung in das Alte Testament* [*An Introduction to the Old Testament*], Tübingen, 1964.

25. Bendavid, Lazarus, in *Neues Theologisches Journal* [*The New Theological Journal*], Nürnberg, 1898.

26. von Däniken, *Der Götterschock.*

27. *Der Grosse Brockhaus* [*German Popular Dictionary*], Wiesbaden, 1954.

28. Salibi, Kamal, *Die Bibel kam aus dem Lande Asir* [*The Bible Originated in the Land of Asir* (Saudi Arabia)], Reinbek bei Hamburg, 1985.

29. *Der Spiegel* No. 39 / 1985, "Hat die Bibel doch nicht Recht?" ["Was the Bible Wrong?"]

30. Wüstenfeld, Ferdinand, *Geschichte der Stadt Medina* [*A History of the City of Medina*], Göttingen, 1860.

31. von Däniken, Erich, *Wir alle sind Kinder der Götter* [Not available in English], Munich, 1987.

32. Ginzberg, *The Legends of the Jews.*

33. *Enzyklopädie des Islam,* Band II [*Encyclopedia of Islam,* Vol. II], Leiden; Leipzig, 1927.

34. Janssen, Enno, "Testament Abrahams" in *Unterweisung in lehrhafter Form. Jüdische Schriften,* Band II [*The Testament of Abraham, in Lessons in Easy Steps. Jewish Texts,* Vol. II], Gütersloh, 1975.

35. Falk-Ronne, Arne, *Auf Abrahams Spuren* [*On Abraham's Trail*], Graz, 1971.

36. Salibi, *Die Bibel kam aus dem Lande Asir.*

37. Lury, Joseph, *Geschichte der Edomiter im biblischen Zeitalter. Inaugural-Dissertation der philosophischen Fakultät der Universität Bern* [*The History of the Edomites in the Biblical Age. Inaugural Dissertation of the Philosophical Faculty of the University of Bern*], Berlin, 1896.

38. Becker, Jürgen, "Die Testamente der zwölf Patriarchen" in *Unterweisung in lehrhafter Form. Jüdische Schriften*, Band III ["The Testaments of the Twelve Patriarchs," in *Lessons in Easy Steps. Jewish Texts*, Vol. III], Gütersloh, 1974.

39. Rahner, *Herders Theologisches Lexicon.*

40. Krassa, Peter, *Gott kam von den Sternen* [*God Came from the Stars*], Vienna, 1969.

41. Rahner, *Herders Theologisches Lexicon.*

42. Davies, Paul, *Die letzten drei Minuten* [*The Last Three Minutes*], Munich, 1996.

43. de Chardin, P. T., *The Phenomenon of Man* [Engl. Translation], William Collins Sons, London, 1959.

44. Puccetti, Roland, *Ausserirdische Intelligenz* [*Extraterrestrial Intelligence*], Düsseldorf, 1970.

CHAPTER 2

1. Bertone, Tarcisio, *Die Botschaft von Fátima* [*The Message of Fátima*], published by the Congregation for the Teaching of the Faith, Vatican City, June 29, 2000.

2. Bertone, *Die Botschaft von Fátima.*

3. Fiebag, Johannes and Peter, *Die geheime Botschaft von Fátima* [*The Secret Message of Fátima*], Tübingen, 1986.

4. Bertone, *Die Botschaft von Fátima.*

5. Rahner, Karl, *Herders Theologisches Lexicon* [*Herders' Theological Encyclopedia*, Vol. I], Freiburg, Basel, Vienna, 1972.

6. von Däniken, Erich, *Der Jüngste Tag hat längst begonnen*, Munich, 1995. [Available in English as *The Return of the Gods*, Chrysalis Vega, London, 2002.]

7. Delitzsch, Fr., *Die grosse Täuschung* [*The Great Hoax*], Stuttgart, Berlin, 1921.

8. Kehl, Robert, *Die Religion des modernen Menschen* [*The Religion of Modern Man*], in *Stiftung für universelle Religion* [*Corporation for Universal Religion*], Heft, 6a, Zurich.

9. *Der Koran. Das heilige Buch des Islam* [*The Koran. The Holy Book of Islam*], Munich, 1964.

10. *Die Welt*, No. 208-36, September 6, 2000, "Die Katholische Kirche erklärt sich für einzigartig—EKD empört" [The Catholic Church Declares Itself Unique—The EKD (Evangelical Churches of Germany) Indignant].

11. Focus, No. 37 / 2000, "Ganze Grösse von Gottes Wort" ["The Greatness of God's Word"].

12. Algermassen, Konrad (et al.), *Lexikon der Marienkunde* [*A Dictionary of the Cult of Mary*], Regensburg, 1957.

13. Apio, Garcia, *Bodas de ouro de Fátima* [*The Golden Weddings of Fátima*], Lisbon, 1967.

14. Renault, Gilbert, *Fátima, esperanca do mundo* [*Fátima, Hope of the World*], Paris, 1957.

15. *Welt am Sonntag,* No. 30, July 25, 1999, "Der Papst verkün-
det des Paradies neu" ["The Pope Announces a New
Paradise"].

16. Aus dem Tagebuch von Johannes XXIII vom 17
August 1959. Audienzen P. Philippe, Kommisar des
Hl. Offiziums [From the Diary of John XXIII of 17
August 1959].

17. Generalaudienz vom 14 Oktober 1981 über "das Ere-
ignis vom Mai" [General Audience of 14 October
1981 Regarding the "Event of May"] in *Insegnamenti di
Giovanni Paolo II* [*Instructions of Giovanni Paulo II*], *IV, 2,*
Cittá del Vaticano 1981.

18. *Der Spiegel,* No. 51 / 1983, "Dir, o Mutter ganz zu eigen"
[article about St. Mary].

19. Bertone, *Die Botschaft von Fátima.*

20. Bertone, *Die Botschaft von Fátima.*

21. Tengg, Franz, *Ich bin die geheimnisvolle Rose* ["I Am the
Mystic Rose"], Vienna, 1973.

22. Apparitions of Mary in Montichiari and Fontanelle,
(Immaculata), Lucerne, 1967.

23. Speelmann, E., *Belgium Marianum,* Paris, 1859.

24. Haesle, Maria, *Eucharistische Wunder aus aller Welt* [*Miracles of the Eucharist Around the World*], Zürich, 1968.

25. Mensching, Gustav, *Die Söhne Gottes aus den heiligen
Schriften der Menschheit* [*The Sons of God from the Holy Texts
of Humankind*], Wiesbaden.

26. *Welt am Sonntag*, No. 36, September 3, 2000, "Marienerscheinungen am Nil" ["Apparitions of St. Mary on the Nile"].

27. Küng, Hans, *Unfehlbar? Eine unerledigte Anfrage* [*Infallible? An Unanswered Question*], Munich, Zurich, 1989.

28. Drewermann, Eugen, *Der Sechste Tag. Die Herkunft des Menschen und die Frage nach Gott* [*The Sixth Day. The Origins of Man and the Question of God*], Zurich, Düsseldorf, 1998.

29. Drewermann, Eugen, and Biser, Eugen, *Welches Credo?* [*Which Credo?*], Basel, Vienna, 1993.

30. Fiebag, Johannes, *Die Anderen. Begegnungen mit einer ausserirdischen Intelligenz* [*The Others. Meetings with an Extraterrestrial Intelligence*], Munich, 1993.

31. Fiebag, *Die Anderen*.

32. Fiebag, *Die Anderen*.

33. Augstein, Rudolf, *Jesus Menschensohn* [*Jesus, Son of Man*], Munich, 1972.

34. Lehmann, Johannes, *Jesus Report*, Düsseldorf, 1970.

35. Carmichael, Joel, *Leben und Tod des Jesus von Nazareth* [*The Life and Death of Jesus of Nazareth*], Munich, 1965.

CHAPTER 3

1. Ludu, Hla, *Folk Tales of Burma*, Mandalay, 1978.

2. Krassa, Peter, *Als die gelben Götter kamen* [*When the Yellow Gods Came*], Munich, 1973.

3. Gould, Charles, *Mythical Monsters*, London, 1886.

4. Kohlenberg, Karl F., *Enträtselte Vorzeit* [*Prehistory Deciphered*], Munich, 1970.

5. Klein, Wilhelm, and Pfannmüller, Günter, *Birma* [*Burma*], Munich, 1996.

6. Aung, Htin, *Burmese Monk's Tales*, London, 1966.

7. Preuss, Theodor Konrad, *Forschungsreise zu den Kagaba* [*An Expedition to the Kagaba*], Vienna, 1926.

8. Preuss, *Forschungsreise zu den Kagaba.*

9. Reichel-Dolmatoff, Gerardo, "Die Kogi in Kolumbien" ["The Kogi of Colombia"], in *Bild der Völker* [*Picture of the People*], Vol. V, Wiesbaden.

10. von Däniken, Erich, *Die Strategie der Götter* [Not available in English], Düsseldorf, 1982.

11. von Däniken, Erich, *Der Jüngste Tag hat längst begonnen*, Munich, 1995. [Available in English as *The Return of the Gods*, Chrysalis Vega, London, 2002.]

12. Klein and Pfannmüller, *Birma.*

13. Rassat, Hans-Joachim, *Ganesa—Eine Untersuchung über Herkunft, Wesen und Kult der elefantenköpfigen Gottheit Indiens* [*Ganesha—An Investigation into the Origins, Nature and Cult of the Elephant-Headed God of India*] (Dissertation), Tübingen, 1955.

14. Fiebag, Peter, *Geheimnisse der Naturvölker* [*Secrets of Native Peoples*], Munich, 1999.

15. Fiebag, *Geheimnisse der Naturvölker.*

CHAPTER 4

1. Bharadwaaji, Maharshi, *Vymaanika-Shaastra.* Translated by Joyser, G. R. Mysore, 1973.

2. Kanjilal, Dileep Kumar, *Vimana in Ancient India.* Calcutta, 1991.

3. Ludwig, A., *Abhandlungen über das Ramayana und die Beziehungen desselben zum Mahabharata* [*Treatises on the Ramayana and Its Connections with the Mahabharata*]. Prague, 1894.

4. Jacobi, Hermann, *Das Ramayana* [*The Ramayana*], Bonn, 1893.

5. Roy, Potrap Chandra, *The Mahabharata,* Calcutta, 1896.

6. Dutt, M. Nath, *The Ramayana,* Calcutta, 1891.

7. Gentes, Lutz, *Die Wirklichkeit der Götter* [*The Reality of the Gods*], Munich, 1996.

8. Risi, Armin, *Gott und die Götter. Das vedische Weltvild revolutioniert die moderne Wissenschaft, Esoterik und Theologie* [*God and the Gods. The Vedic World View Revolutionizes Modern Science, Esotericism and Theology*], Zurich, 1995.

9. Roy, *The Mahabharata,* 1896.

10. Mani, Vaidhyanathan, Raja, *The Cult of Weapons,* Delhi, 1985.

11. Laufer, Berthold, "The Prehistory of Aviation" in *Field Museum of Natural History,* Anthropological Series Vol. XVIII, No. 1, Chicago, 1928.

12. Mani, Raja, *The Cult of Weapons.*

13. Roy, Potrap Chandra, *The Mahabharata, section Vana Parva,* Calcutta, 1884.

14. Eiseley, Loren, *Von der Entstehung des Lebens und der Natur- geschichte des Menschen* [*On the Origins of Life and the Natural History of Humans*], Munich, 1959.

15. Mani, *Raja, The Cult of Weapons.*

16. Roy, *The Mahabharata, section Vana Parva.*

17. Roy, Potrap Chandra, *The Mahabharata,* Vol. VI, Drona Parva, Calcutta, 1893.

18. Roy, Biren, *Das Mahabharata—ein altindisches Epos aus dem Englischen übertragen von E. Roemer* [*The Mahabharata—an Ancient Indian Epic, translated from English by E. Roemer*], Düsseldorf, 1961.

19. Roy, *The Mahabharata,* Calcutta, 1891.

20. Burckhardt, Georg, *Gilgamesch—eine Erzählung aus dem alten Orient* [*Gilgamesh—A Tale from the Ancient Orient*], Wiesbaden, 1958.

21. Bhandakar Oriental Research Institute, Vana Parva, Calcutta, 1981.

22. *Abhandlungen der philosophisch-philologischen Klasse der Königlich Bayerischen Akademie der Wissenschaften.* 23. Band, 1. Abteilung, Kebra Negest, die Herrlichkeit der Könige. [*Treatises of the Philosophical-Philological Class of the Royal Bavarian Academy of Sciences,* Vol. XXIII, Section 1. Kebra Negest, The Splendor of the Kings], Munich.

23. von Däniken, Erich, *Der Götterschock* [Not available in English], Munich, 1992.

24. Grassmann, Hermann, *Rig-Veda*, Leipzig, 1876.

25. Deussen, Paul, *Sechzig Upanishads des Veda* [*Sixty Upanishads from the Vedas*], Leipzig, 1905.

26. Zick, Michael, *Das Geheimnis des begrabenen Tempels* [*The Mystery of the Buried Temple*], in *Bild der Wissenschaft* [*Picture of Science*], No. 1, 1997.

27. Zick, *Das Geheimnis des begrabenen Tempels*.

28. von Däniken, Erich, *Der Jüngste Tag hat längst begonnen*, Munich, 1995. [Available in English as *The Return of the Gods*, Chrysalis Vega, London, 2002.]

29. Wilson, Robert Anton, *Die neue Inquisition. Irationaler Rationalismus und die Zitadelle der Wissenschaft*, Frankfurt, 1992. [Available in English as *The New Inquisition. Irrational Rationalism and the Citadel of Science*, New Falcon Publications, Tempe, Arizona, USA, 1986.]

30. BBC London, Television programs, *Horizon*, October 28, 1999—"Atlantis Uncovered" and *Horizon*, November 4, 1999—"Atlantis Reborn."

31. Bauval, Robert, and Gilbert, Adrian, *The Orion Mystery*, Heinemann, London, 1994.

32. *Bild der Wissenschaft* online, newsticker of December 2, 2000, "Ägyptische Behörden verhindern in letzter Minute Gentests an den Mumien von Tutenchamun und Amenhotep III" ["Egyptian Authorities' Last-Minute Stop on Genetic Tests of the Mummies of Tutankhamun and Amenhotep III"].

33. Vyasadevas, Srila, "Srimad-Bhagavatam" [translated by A. C. Bahktivedanta Swami Prabhupada] in *Krsna, die Quelle*

aller Freude, Vol. II [*Krsna (Krishna), the Source of All Joy,* Vol. II], Vienna, 1987.

34. Rao, S. R., *The Lost City of Dvaraka* [Dwarka], New Delhi, 1999.

35. Rao, *The Lost City of Dvaraka.*

36. Wright, Giles, "The Riddle of the Sands" in *New Scientist,* July 10, 1999.

37. Daubree, M., "On the Substances Obtained from Some "Forts Vitrifies" [Vitrified Forts] in France," in *American Journal of Science,* Vol. III, No. 22, 1881.

38. Childress, David Hatcher, *Technology of the Gods, the Incredible Science of the Ancients,* Kempton, Illinois, 2000.

39. DiPiettro, Vincent, and Molenaar, Gregory, *Unusual Mars Surface Features.* Fourth edition, Glenndale, Maryland, 1988.

40. *Welt am Sonntag,* No. 41, 1966, "Weider Spuren von Leben in Stein von Mars entdeckt" ["Further Traces of Life Found in Stone from Mars"].

41. Swift, Jonathan, *Gulliver's Travels's,* 1726.

42. Bürgin, Luc, *Mondblitze. Unterdrückte Entdeckungen in Raumfahrt und Wissenschaft* [*Lightning Flashes on the Moon. Suppressed Discoveries in Space Travel and Science*], Munich, 1994.

43. Raghavan, Srinivasa, *The Date of the Mahabharata War,* Madras, 1969.

44. von Däniken, Erich, *Der Tag, an dem die Götter kamen, 11 August 3114 v. Chr.* [*The Day the Gods Came, 11 August, 3114 B.C.*], Munich, 1984.

45. Makemson, Worcester M., *The Book of the Jaguar Priest*. A translation of the *Book of Chilam Balam of Tizimin* with a commentary, New York, 1951.

46. von Däniken, *Der Jüngste Tag hat längst begonnen.*

47. Chargaff, Erwin, *Warnungstafeln. Die Vergangenheit spricht zur Gegenwart* [*Warning Signs. The Past Speaks to the Present*], Stuttgart, 1982.

48. *Focus*, No. 50, 2000, "Sternstunde der Steinzeit" ["A Great Moment in the Stone Age"].

49. *Focus*, No. 50, 2000, "Sternstunde der Steinzeit."

50. von Däniken, Erich, *Im Namen von Zeus*, Munich, 1999. [Available in English as *Odyssey of the Gods*, Chrysalis Vega, London, 2002.]

51. von Däniken, Erich, *Die Steinzeit war ganz anders* [Not available in English], Munich, 1991.

52. Hawkins, Gerald S., *Stonehenge Decoded*, New York, 1965.

53. Meisenheimer, Klaus, *Stonehenge, eine steinerne Finsternisuhr?* [*Stonehenge, a Stone Eclipse Predictor?*] in *Sterne und Weltraum* [*Stars and Space*], SuW-Special No. 4, Heidelberg, 1999.

54. O'Kelly, M., *Newgrange*, London, 1983.

55. Ray, I. P., "The Winter Solstice Phenomenon at Newgrange, Ireland," in *Nature*, January 1989, Vol. 337.

56. von Däniken, *Die Steinzeit war ganz anders.*

57. Mani, V. R., *The Cult of Weapons. The Iconography of the Ayudhapurusas*, Delhi, 1985.

58. Singh, Simon, *Geheime Botschaften* [*Secret Messages*], Frankfurt, a. M., 2000.

59. *Der Spiegel,* No. 50, 1999, "Ahnenpass aus dem Labor" ["Ancestral Passport from the Laboratory"].

60. Rees, Martin, "Hallo, hier Erde—hört da draussen jemand zu?" ["Hello, Earth Calling—Can Anyone Hear Us Out There?"] in *Die Welt,* January 9, 2001.

AFTERWORD

1. *Die Welt,* January 10, 2001, "Neue Erkenntnisse zur Evolution des Menschen" ["New Insights on the Evolution of Humans"].

2. Lossau, Norbert, "Von Bruder zu Bruder" ["From Brother to Brother"] in *Die Welt,* January 12, 2001.

3. Bostanci, Adam, "Evolution durch genetisches Design" ["Evolution by Genetic Design"] in *Die Welt,* January 16, 2001.

INDEX

PHOTO CREDITS

ABOUT THE AUTHOR

Erich von Däniken is arguably the most widely read and most copied nonfiction author in the world. He published his first (and best-known) book, *Chariots of the Gods?*, in 1968. The worldwide bestseller was followed by more than three dozen books, including bestsellers *Confessions of an Egyptologist, War of the Gods, Eyewitness to the Gods, The Gods Never Left Us, Twilight of the Gods, History Is Wrong, Evidence of the Gods, Remnants of the Gods,* and *Odyssey of the Gods*. His works have been translated into twenty-eight languages and have sold more than sixty-five million copies. Several have also been made into films. Von Däniken's ideas have been the inspiration for a wide range of television series, including the History Channel's hit *Ancient Aliens*. His research organization, the AAS-RA/legendarytimes. com (Archaeology, Astronauts and SETI Research Association), comprises laymen and academics from all walks of life. Internationally, there are about 10,000 members. Erich lives in Switzerland but is an ever-present figure on the international lecture circuit, traveling more than 100,000 miles a year.

To follow the latest visit *www.daniken.com/en/* or Erich von Däniken's Official Fan Page on Facebook.

ALSO BY
ERICH VON DANIKEN
FROM NEW PAGE BOOKS

Confessions of an Egyptologist

Enoch and the Return of the Gods

Evidence of the Gods

Evolution Is Wrong

Eyewitness to the Gods

The Gods Never Left Us

History Is Wrong

Odyssey of the Gods

Remnants of the Gods

Twilight of the Gods

War of the Gods